Y0-CCS-544

MAKING YOUR CHURCH GROW

The Role Of Leadership
In Church Growth

BY RICHARD K. SMITH

Fairway Press
Lima, Ohio

MAKING YOUR CHURCH GROW

FIRST EDITION
Copyright © 1992 by
Richard K. Smith

7906 / ISBN 1-55673-446-8

DEDICATED

to

Dr. Marvin W. Gongre who persistently encouraged and prodded me to do the research
and writing for this book

and

My wife **Janet** who has stood by me in the effort
to have this book published

and

My friend and Savior **Jesus** who died that His body
the Church would grow and reflect His grace
and truth around the world among all peoples.

Table Of Contents

Summary

The Function Of Leadership In Church Growth

The basic objectives of this book are four-fold. The first objective is the attempt to clearly articulate the principle that the Church's leadership plays a major role in church growth. The second objective is to show historically from Scripture and church history that the leadership of the Church has performed an outstanding ministry in the expansion of the body of Christ around the world. The third objective involves the methodological approach that seeks to analyze the various ways in which the Church's leadership can pursue the cause of church growth. Fourthly, there is a motivational objective to inspire and challenge the Church's leadership to take the responsibility of working for church growth.

This book approaches the topic in the following manner:

A. Chapter one is introductory and foundational. It notes the fact that the Church is experiencing unusual growth in many corners of the globe. There is a brief definition of church growth as it is generally understood today. Leadership is identified as one of the key factors influencing church growth. The chapter points out the urgency of the leadership need in the Church, for without it the Church cannot develop and grow as it should. Finally, leadership is identified as a key church growth principle that plays an indispensable role in affecting other church growth factors.

B. The second chapter surveys the definition of leadership, particularly, the definition of a church growth leader. There is a brief exploration of secular leadership theory followed by a Biblical view of the subject. The secular and Biblical views are compared in order to contrast the humanistic idea of secular leadership with the Biblical viewpoint which centers on service for the glory of God and the expansion of His Church.

7

C. The third chapter examines the theology of church growth leadership. The attempt is made to show that God has chosen to use individuals for the accomplishment of His purposes in the world. The chapter sets forth how Christ chose, discipled, and trained certain men to participate in the building of His Church. It further shows how the Holy Spirit ordains and equips leaders with spiritual gifts for leadership ministries in the Church and the world. The chapter concludes that there is the divine design of God to use certain believers to lead the Church in its expansion.

D. The fourth chapter sets forth a brief history of the involvement of leaders who have had a vital role in the growth of the Church. It first of all notes how leadership has been a key component in growing religious movements. Then a few select case studies are presented to illustrate how leaders have had such a major part in growing congregations. Finally there is a brief look at how leaders through the centuries have rendered an important service in the Church's expansion around the world.

E. The fifth chapter examines the need for preparing leaders to achieve effective church growth expertise. This section looks at the need of and the demand for trained leadership in order that the Church may experience impressive growth. Then there is an examination of the various types of leaders that the Church needs in order to be healthy and to expand. Finally the point is made that curriculum and the model of theological education must be designed to serve the maximum growth of the Church.

F. The sixth chapter examines the role that leaders have in the organization of the Church. The chapter looks at the distinctive function that denominational and mission leaders, pastors, and lay leaders exercise at each particular level of the Church. It is further presented that the role these leaders play is to administer with a clear design for church growth.

G. The seventh chapter centers its attention on the task of leadership in church growth. The chapter first examines the spiritual qualities and leadership abilities that leadership must possess in order to be equipped for the performance of the task implicit in church growth. The second significant portion of the chapter takes a look at the various kinds of key functions that the Church's leadership, particularly pastors, must carry out that will assist the Church to grow.

H. The eighth chapter concludes the study. This chapter leaves a final challenge to the Church's leaders to accept the immense responsibility of working for church growth. It also attempts to alert the leadership of the Church to the great opportunity that exists to be involved in leading the body of Christ in ever increasing expansion.

CHAPTER I

The Importance Of Leadership In Church Growth

God desires and intends His Church to grow. Increase in the number of believers and development of their spiritual growth are among the Church's highest priorities. There are a multitude of causes that contribute to the growth of the Church. It is evident that the leadership of the Church plays a major role in the dynamics of church growth. Thus, in light of more than three billion unreached people in the world at the end of this century, it is vital that the dynamics of leadership in church growth be studied in a more detailed analysis.

The Growing Church In The World Today

Churches around the world are experiencing significant growth. In spite of world confusion, churches continually report exciting growth statistics. The Church is reaching greater numbers of homogeneous units for Christ. The Church in Latin America continues to experience rapid growth. Sub-Saharan Africa has become substantially Christian. Even Churches in past and present communist nations are reporting growth. Lois

McKinney summarizes the church growth picture by stating that in:

> *Some places church growth may be painstakingly slow; in others it may be breathtakingly fast. In widely scattered places, through diverse means, and among hundreds of different peoples, Christ is building up His Church.* [1]

Two church growth specialists, Donald McGavran and Winfield Arn, have noted that the Church today is faced with unprecedented receptivity to the message of Christ. They observe that nations and tribes of the world are more responsive to the Gospel than they have ever been before. [2] The leadership of the Church is responsible for leading God's people into the harvest.

In addition to winning the lost and edifying believers, the Church and its leadership are faced with many other challenges. There are the internal challenges of raising church budgets, building bigger and better buildings, paving the parking lot, organizing committees, and many more. And then there are the external challenges of building better race relations, assisting the poor, finding homes and jobs for refugees, teaching the illiterates, working with underprivileged youth, seeking for more equitable justice, pushing for world peace, and scores of others. The bottom line to all of this according to today's foremost missiologist, Donald McGavran, is that:

> *. . . for the welfare of the world, for the good of mankind — according to the Bible, one task is paramount. Today's supreme task is effective multiplication of churches in the receptive societies of earth.* [3]

The growing Church today must keep before itself the supreme Christological mandate of making disciples of all peoples. Fulfilling this mandate is the supreme purpose which should guide the entire mission, establish its priorities, and coordinate all its activities. All of the good things that the

Church does must contribute to, and not crowd out, reconciliation of men to God in the Church of Jesus Christ. In speaking to the issue of the Church's priority in mission Donald McGavran states:

> *The Lord Jesus put it succinctly when He said, "Seek ye first the kingdom of God and His righteousness and all these things shall be added to you." He spoke of food and clothing, the simplest necessities of life, but the passage will bear much added freight: safety, health, education, comfort, production — even justice, peace, and brotherhood. As we try to help men to achieve these, the longest first step we can lead them to take is to believe in Christ as Lord and Savior and become dependable members of His Church. Enormous liberation of the human spirit and extension of righteousness among men will become possible as sound churches of Christ are multiplied among the three billion who now yield Him no allegiance. Such liberated persons and congregations will become in their own cultures and communities the most effective and permanent sources of "good works" as well as of true cooperation toward solving the bitter practical problems of the world.*[4]

There are some areas of the world where there is little or no church growth. In some cases repressive political regimes and fanatical religious systems hinder church growth. In most cases, however, the lack of church growth is remediable. As if addressing the Church's leadership in this regard, McGavran notes that:

> *Arrested growth can be ascribed to faulty procedures. Sometimes, when a shepherd returns empty-handed, it is because the sheep refuse to be found and flee at his approach. Sometimes, however, empty-handedness becomes a habit and is caused by peering into ravines where there are no sheep, resolutely neglecting those who long to be found in favor of those who refuse to be. Sometimes it is a question of sticking for decades to methods which*

13

have proved ineffective. Suffice it to say that lack of church growth is an unnecessary trait, or experience, of many branches of the church and many missionary societies.[5]

It is urgent that Church leaders awaken to the fact that the Church now faces a most responsive world. Together with lack of growth in far too many cases goes an amazing amount of real, sometimes spectacular, growth in other cases. There are few nations "where there is not some receptive segment of the population . . . . There are more winnable people in the world today than ever before."[6] How many of these winnable people are won to Christ and brought into the Church will depend a great deal upon the leadership at every level of the Church around the world.

The Church Growth Movement has become a recognized body of thought. Leaders in many countries have come to share in church growth thinking. Church leaders and pastors are using different emphases to fit many different situations, and as a result they are seeing their sections of God's Church grow.

Toward A Definition Of Church Growth

Church growth thinking has attracted the attention of Church leaders around the world. Even a few years ago, few people had heard the term "church growth." Today the term is a part of standard theological vocabulary. Many segments of the Church around the world "can now give testimony that Church Growth thinking brings growth."[7]

Donald McGavran and Winfield Arn have defined church growth as

> *. . . an application of biblical, theological, anthropological, and sociological principles to congregations and denominations and to their communities in an effort to disciple the greatest number of people for Jesus Christ.*

14

Believing that "it is God's will that His Church grow and His lost children be found," Church Growth endeavors to devise strategies, develop objectives, and apply proven principles of growth to individual congregations, to denominations, and to the worldwide Body of Christ.[8]

They further define a church growth principle as

. . . a universal truth which, when properly interpreted and applied, contributes significantly to the growth of churches and denominations. It is a truth of God which leads his church to spread his Good News, plant church after church, and increase his Body.[9]

A church growth principle is discovered by careful observation. One must ask why the growth occured. First of all it is important to observe what God is doing. There may be a particular situation or situations that God is using to bring growth. Secondly, and equally important, one must observe what the believers, and the leadership in particular, are doing to promote this growth. Carefully analyzed findings lead to one or more church growth principles. In searching for church growth principles McGavran and Arn caution that

*. . . it is important to find **real** reasons. Often superficial explanations obscure basic principles. A good researcher digs to bedrock. Many reasons for church growth are alleged. They represent an erroneous judgment or, more frequently, a partial judgment. They take one cause for church growth and state it as if it were the **only** cause.*[10]

McGavran and Arn also note that church growth principles are generally applicable worldwide. Church growth principles hurdle cultural and geographic barriers because the Church is made up of people as the common element.[11] One very important church growth principle that will be investigated by this book is the major role the Church's leadership plays in the growth of the Church or in its lack of growth. It is clearly evident from research that growth, or even non-growth, is greatly affected by the Church's leadership. It is possible that church leaders around the world from varying cultures and speaking many different languages can be instrumental, through different emphases adapted to differing situations, in seeing their parts of God's church grow.

Some view church growth as being only concerned with adding more members to the church roll. However, church growth can be viewed from several different perspectives. In an interview the eminent missiologist, Peter Wagner, noted that church growth has four dimensions. He articulated the four dimensions in the following manner:

> In commending the church at Jerusalem, chapter two of Acts says that church growth is to **grow up** in our personal and corporate spiritual life; the church at Jerusalem matured in its understanding of apostolic teaching by gathering together for the breaking of the bread, prayer, and fellowship. Second, they **grew together**. In fact, the Jerusalem church lived together in a community; they weren't "lone-ranger" Christians. Third, they **grew out**. They did not exist for themselves; they reached out into the community and performed works of charity, which in turn, created a favorable impression of the church in its neighbors' minds. And fourth, they **grew in numbers**. As a result of the way those people lived, the Lord added daily to the church such as should be saved. A church that is pleasing to God grows in these four ways.[12]

There were many factors that contributed to the early church growing in these four dimensions. Primary factors were the life and dynamic of the Holy Spirit. Another key factor was the leadership of certain individuals who became gifted leaders through the ministry of the Holy Spirit.

These four dimensions of growth, as articulated by Wagner, have been expressed with different terminology by several noted scholars.[13] The "growing up" is maturational growth which concerns qualitative perfection or maturity. Maturational

16

growth is both behavioral and conceptual. Having the mind of Christ and exhibiting his holy life are the goals of this internal, qualitative dimension of church growth. The "growing together" is organic growth which has to do with the development of the Church. It involves the internal structure of relationships within the body itself. It includes such areas of the church's life as the development of leadership, the rise and structuring of organization, and other aspects of the church's life that contribute to the qualitative growth of spiritual life. The "growing out" is referred to as incarnational growth which involves the Church in its environment. It involves the Church speaking prophetically to its generation and becoming involved in lifting up the downtrodden and dispossessed. The "growing in numbers" is numerical growth which involves the Church's perpetual ingathering of new disciples of Jesus Christ into the fellowship of local congregations or the gathering of new believers into new churches.[14] Dynamic leadership is absolutely mandatory if the Church is going to grow in each of these four dimensions. Such growth does not just happen. It only happens through the Spirit-empowered and designed leadership of men and women.

To look at church growth from a slightly different perspective it can be viewed from four other dimensions. These four dimensions have been termed "kinds" of church growth and are briefly described as follows:

> *Internal growth* is growth in grace and takes place when the church is edified. *Expansion growth* is the numerical increase of a local congregation. *Extension growth* is one church planting a daughter church in another community, among people socially and culturally like the mother church. *Bridging growth* is one church planting a daughter church across significant cultural barriers.[15]

Again, the Church can only experience significant growth in each of these dimensions as there is dynamic involvement of the Church's leadership.

17

A great deal of the church growth emphasis has been centered on numerical additions of new disciples of Jesus Christ to the Church. But there needs to be no apology for focusing on this aspect of the growth of the Church. This is the one dimension of church growth that is absolutely essential to all the rest. Charles Chaney and Ron Lewis in *Design for Church Growth* state the issue clearly when they state:

> *There can be no perfecting of the saints without saints. No organic growth can take place without the building blocks with which to develop structure. Real substance, actual quantity, is prerequisite to the incarnation of a church in the culture where it is planted and the molding of society after the image of Christ.*
>
> *Numerical growth is fundamental and integral to God's intention to take from "among the nations a people" for himself (Acts 15:14). Numerical growth is, therefore, the essential and irreplaceable element in the mission of the church. A church is not fulfilling its mission, is not obedient to that for which it is sent, if it is not making disciples to Jesus Christ and planting churches within each and every ethnic segment of society. We can know how faithful we are being to God in this regard.* [16]

The goal is that there be a living body of believers under the banner of Jesus Christ in every segment of society on earth. Every society should be throbbing with Christian life, full of groups of committed Christians, loving, serving, praying, growing in the Word, reaching out. [17] In a world of approximately 5.4 billion people it is imperative that godly men and women lead and galvanize the Church around the world to have this absolute perspective of church growth firmly in mind and exhibited in action. This perspective of church growth is related directly to the will of God. Therefore any Church leader, at any level of the Church, or a local congregation anywhere in the world, that is not concerned with growth and discipleship, is really disobeying God and is doing what is not pleasing to God. [18]

As church growth thinking has developed and come into its own as a missiological science, church leaders have raised questions regarding its distinctiveness. While the Church experienced a dramatic reformation in its theology during the sixteenth century the Church has not really experienced a dramatic reformation in its mission until church growth thinking was developed during the second half of this twentieth century. George Hunter has come to the conviction that church growth represents an historic new departure for what he calls "informed evangelization." As an advocate of church growth Hunter suggests that the church growth approach has a dozen distinctives which are:

> *1. In church growth thought, the objective of evangelizing is to "make disciples," actual followers of Jesus Christ, biblically rooted and incorporated into the Body of Christ. The motive for making new disciples is not self-aggrandizement, but faithfulness to God.*
>
> *2. Church growth takes statistics and graphs seriously in analyzing the past record and present situation, and in planning for new church growth.*
>
> *3. Church growth regards goal setting as an indispensable part of a congregation's planned approach to outreach.*
>
> *4. Church growth people know that no one method of evangelism will engage and elicit response from men and women of all cultures and subcultures. The Church must fashion methods that are indigenous to target populations and effective in them.*
>
> *5. Church growth harnesses the social sciences, especially sociology and cultural anthropology, to develop strategy for the missionary task.*
>
> *6. Church growth leaders emphasize practical research to gain the facts needed for developing evangelism theory and planning for effective Christian expansion.*
>
> *7. Church growth research constantly tests inherited evangelistic principles and methods and discovers new ones.*
>
> *8. Church growth people believe that because of God's prevenient grace, great numbers are receptive. Church*

*growth research has discovered **indicators** to enable us to perceive those who might welcome the Gospel and become dependable members of Christ's Church.*

9. Church growth emphasizes extensive, even "extravagant," new church planting, believing the Christian movement needs 300,000 more churches in the United States.

10. Church growth strategists now have at their disposal a worldwide data base from church growth research, upon which to predicate theory and strategy.

11. Church growth people hold a high doctrine of the Church, believing that the folding of people into Christ's flock is an essential part of their evangelization.

12. Church growth people are confident that the growth of Christ's Church among the peoples of the earth is the will of God, and he is present to empower her outreach and expansion.[19]

If these church growth distinctives involve "informed evangelization" it means that someone in the Church must be informed. The most likely core of individuals in the Church that need this information are its leaders. The leaders themselves must be informed concerning church growth principles so that they can pass them on to the Church's membership. The leaders then can arouse the Church to a new awareness of the urgency of finding those potent combinations that God uses to bring growth to His Church.

The Leadership Factor In Church Growth

Church growth can be viewed and studied from four different dimensions. The first is the dimension of the context and culture. The growth of the Church will be affected by the particular society and culture in which it finds itself. How churches relate to and react with the local context and culture will have great bearing on the rate of church growth. Another dimension of church growth involves methodology. The mix of methodologies will have a great impact upon the response and growth that will result. A key emphasis of church growth is to study growth patterns to discover the effectiveness of various methodologies so as to arrange and rearrange methodologies for maximum effectiveness. A third dimension of church growth involves personnel. The Church will not achieve significant growth in a context and culture unless there is active participation of the human factor. Methodologies are only fruitful when put into action by the human factor. The key human factor in church growth is without question the leadership of the Church. The membership of the Church is not likely to be actively involved in church growth in a dynamic way unless the leaders of the Church inspire, train, and pave the way. The crucial factor of leadership in church growth is made very clear by the history of the early Church. The fourth dimension of church growth is that of the divine. Without the ministry and dynamic of the Holy Spirit there can be no church growth. It is God that gives the increase when all other factors, including leadership, are in place. The Book of Acts gives a very clear record of the indispensable ministry of the Holy Spirit in the growth of the Church. Of these four dimensions of church growth the third dimension of leadership is the aspect of church growth which is the concern of this book. The dimensions of context and culture, methodology, and the divine, have been given considerable attention in church growth thinking and literature. The dimension of leadership, for some unknown reason, has been given only cursory attention.

It has been observed by Peter Wagner that there are four dimensions to missions. The first dimension is that of height and involves the relationship of people to God, reconciliation, and the new birth. The second dimension is depth and involves personal holiness and the Spirit-filled life. The third dimension is breadth and involves witnessing and sharing Christ with those who are not yet Christians. Wagner states that all three dimensions are essential to missions but that there is an equally essential fourth dimension, namely, strategy. Wagner then divides strategy into four areas. These areas are first, right goals; second, the right place at the right time; third, the right methods; and fourth, the right people.[20] Strategy in church growth involves the right people. In particular it involves the leadership of the Church. God brings the harvest to ripeness, but He does not do the harvesting. He uses His laborers to accomplish this task.[21] The Church today desperately needs leaders who will lead the way into the harvest fields of responsive peoples.

Church leaders may give various answers as to why they are involved in a leadership role. The most basic reason should be to glorify God. Some leaders may see leading their congregation in meaningful worship as important. Some leaders put their emphasis on a ministry of preaching and teaching to build up the body of believers. There are those who see the smooth operation of the Church's organization as a very important function. Some Church leaders may see their leadership role as assisting in reaching out from the Church to be involved in the social welfare of the community. One function of Church leadership, that is often overlooked or downplayed, is to focus on church growth. In a broad sense church growth means improving the spiritual quality of the believers in the Church, but it is also concerned with a consistent and sustained increase in the number of believers.[22]

The Leadership Crisis In Church Growth

LeRoy Eims in the preface of his book, *Be the Leaders You Were Meant to Be*, notes that "a crisis of leadership engulfs the world." He further notes that "men who know the way and can lead others on the right path are few."[23] John English in his book, *The Minister and His Ministry*, states that "an army is as good as its officers."[24] Church growth is urgently dependent upon the Church's leadership. If the Church's leaders are in tune with church growth and give leadership to its implementation, the believers in the pew will certainly follow and become involved. The performance of leaders and laity in the church may be hard to measure in every respect. The

22

bottom line always belongs to God because spiritual results cannot always be measured by human instruments. But even though this be the case, it is very clear in Scripture that a leader is expected to be performance-minded and results-oriented.

J. Oswald Sanders in his book, *Spiritual Leadership*, states that the "supernatural nature of the church demands a leadership that rises above the human."[25] Sanders notes further that there has never been a greater need for God-anointed and God-mastered individuals to meet this crucial need of leadership. It may well be that this type of leadership has been in short supply for the simple reason that its demands are far too stringent. This crisis in need of leadership is stated clearly by Sanders when he says:

> *The overriding need of the church, if it is to discharge its obligation to the rising generation, is for a leadership that is authoritative, spiritual, and sacrificial. Authoritative, because people love to be led by one who knows where he is going and who inspires confidence. They follow almost without question the man who shows himself wise and strong, who adheres to what he believes. Spiritual, because a leadership that is unspiritual, that can be fully explained in terms of the natural, although ever so attractive and competent, will result only in sterility and moral and spiritual bankruptcy. Sacrificial, because modeled on the life of the One who gave Himself a sacrifice for the whole world, who left us an example that we should follow His steps.[26]*

The Church can always expect to grow in the most healthy way when it is blessed with strong, spiritual leaders who expect and experience the manifestation of the supernatural in their service. Growing churches are not led by church committees and councils. They are led by very dynamic, Spirit-filled, enthusiastic, and intense individuals.[27]

The Leadership Principle in Church Growth

Almost all who examine church growth conclude that the key of keys, the master key as it were, is leadership. Delos Miles in *Church Growth — A Mighty River* states this issue very clearly when he says that "If a church has the right kind of leaders, and the right amount of leaders, other factors being balanced, it will grow.[28] David Hesselgrave speaks to the importance of the leadership principle when he states that "there must be much more strategic thinking and serious direction on the part of those who have been duly appointed as leaders of the Church.[29] Hesselgrave notes further that there needs to be a much more disciplined involvement "if we are ever to accomplish what should be accomplished in the time that remains to us to obey our commission and complete our mission."[30]

The leadership principle is crucial to church growth. Unless there is a core of those individuals who take the lead in working for growth in the Church, it is almost certain that the growth will be minimal, or at least not up to the standard that God would desire. The tendency for the Church's leadership is to function primarily as caretakers of the churches already established. One of the most important functions of the Church's leadership is not only to encourage but suggest ways and means of achieving greater church growth. Someone, namely the leadership, has to project a master plan and gather the resources that will contribute to growth. The people in the pew are often available for the cause of church growth if only the leadership will show the way.

The leadership principle is also important because God wants and intends His Church to grow. This is not a debatable issue for God sent His Son to redeem the lost, and thus Christ declared, "I will build my church; and the gates of hell shall not prevail against it" (Matthew 16:18b). The Christological mandate to make disciples of all the nations was in order to build the Church, and this mandate was channeled through a core of leaders that Christ had specifically trained for a leadership role. It is clear that God works through individuals of His choice to accomplish His purposes. God chooses, equips, and commissions certain individuals to work as undershepherds. God's instruments to build His Church are people.[31] The principle of leadership is most basic to the building and growth of the Church.

24

The Leadership Mainspring In Church Growth

As we inquire into the factors that contribute to church growth it is quickly evident that the principle of leadership is positively crucial for significant growth. Leadership as a mainspring is a principle or most compelling cause of church growth. David Hesselgrave in the final chapter of *Dynamic Religious Movements* analyzes what causes religious movements to grow, and in that chapter he discusses four basic types of causes which he summarizes as follows:

> *(1) A necessary cause is one that must occur if (in this case) religious growth is to occur.*
> *(2) A sufficient cause is one that is always followed by growth.*
> *(3) A contributory cause is one that makes it likely that growth will occur. (It is only one of multiple factors which may produce growth.)*
> *(4) A contingent cause is a factor that makes it possible for another factor to function as a contributory cause.* [32]

Hesselgrave notes that it is important to distinguish the various types of causation and that numerous churches fail in this regard. [33] Our task of participation and responsibility in the building of the Church of Christ will be greatly clarified if we recognize the leadership as a mainspring of church growth.

A necessary cause for church growth is that the people of God go forth to preach the gospel faithfully in accordance with His command (Romans 10:13-15). God in His wisdom has sovereignly designed the way in which men and women are brought into the fellowship of the Church. God's design is that every believer be a faithful messenger of the Gospel through which men and women will be saved and made a part of the Church. [34] Thus, all believers are responsible to be concerned for and involved in seeking the growth of the Church. From this standpoint it could be said that the function of leadership in church growth is not a necessary cause. In looking at leadership in Scripture and the role of leaders as evidenced in church growth case studies, it is clear that the function of leaders in the Church is pivotal in the Church achieving growth that could be termed significant growth. After looking at what causes various religious movements to grow David Hesslegrave concludes that "one is tempted to say that if there is any necessary or sufficient cause for the success of a movement apart from the purely spiritual factors . . . it is that the movement have outstanding leadership."[35] From these perspectives it could be concluded that the function of leadership in achieving significant church growth is without question a necessary cause.

In looking at the function of leadership in church growth it would be imperative that one be more cautious in asserting that leadership is a sufficient cause, that is, that the right kind of Church leadership doing the right things will always result in significant church growth. Leadership would not be a sufficient cause for church growth for two basic reasons. Outstanding leadership is not a sufficient cause of church growth for in some cases there will be outright rejection of the Gospel in which case the Lord instructs his disciples to shake the dust from their feet and leave the town. In some cases there may not be qualitative growth in a church because the believers are resisting a deeper work of the Word and the Spirit in their lives. Another basic reason is that, in a very real sense, the only sufficient cause of the growth of the Church is the sovereign and gracious action of the Triune God and His Word. Hesselgrave elaborates further on this point when he notes that:

> *Our Lord said **he would build his church** and the gates of hell would not prevail against it (Matthew 16:18). When our Lord admonished his disciples to bear much fruit he also reminded them that apart from him they could not do anything (John 15:5). When the greatest "church growth specialist" of them all wrote concerning his role in the growth of the church at Corinth he said, "I planted, Apollos watered, **but God was causing the growth**" (1 Corinthians 3:6, NASB).*[36]

Leadership is clearly a contributory cause of church growth. It is one of multiple factors which may produce growth. For some there may be a tendency to think simplistically of the cause or causes that contribute to church growth when in fact there is a wide variety of possible causes. The realization of church growth is most certainly the result of a multiplicity of causes. Hesselgrave at this point gives some critical words of caution when he states:

> *Failure to understand this simple fact has occasioned the erroneous notion — rife in Christian missions — that there must be **some one key** which unlocks the door to great religious growth. Strategists and practitioners alike have made one false start after another — carefully devising a plan of evangelism and church growth, only to abandon it after a few months or years in favor of another plan that has new promise. The resultant loss of time and effort to Christian missions is incalculable. It would seem far better to recognize that growth is the result of a confluence of factors, and to devise an overall plan which takes as many of them as possible into account. Minor adjustments and innovations will, of course, always be in order. But the disruption that results from repeated backtracking and starting along new paths can be averted only by thinking in terms of **multiple causes**.*[37]

While there are many contributory causes to church growth there are some that are more essential than others. From the Biblical record and numerous case studies it can and has been demonstrated that leadership is one of the extremely essential contributory causes, a point which will be further illustrated in this book. Thus, without apology, it can be stated that leadership in the Church is one of the key contributory causes of church growth.

Leadership in church growth is certainly without question a contingent cause. It is a situation where various factors that favor church growth can take effect or converge in such a way for the cause of growth because the factor of leadership is present to trigger the other causes into action. The leadership factor is an important contingent cause for in many cases growth will be hindered or not even take place unless the leadership factor is present. The function of leadership in the Church is paramount because of the fact that it is a contingent factor upon which other growth factors depend. Without a mainspring a watch cannot function. Leadership is certainly the mainspring of church growth, for it acts as a catalyst that enables other growth-enhancing factors to play their role. The Church is unlikely to experience healthy expansion if the leadership is not committed to the process of church growth.

Leadership As Cause Of Growth And Non-Growth

Many varied factors contribute to church growth. The "mix"[38] of these various factors will vary from congregation to congregation and from place to place. Leadership is clearly recognized as a significant cause of church growth. Unsuitable leadership or the lack of leadership can be a definite cause of non-growth. The lack of certain church growth factors may not adversely affect the rate of church growth although their presence may enhance the rate. But leadership is one of those church growth ingredients that has such a decisive impact on church growth that unsuitable leadership or the lack of it will contribute significantly to a lack of growth or to a complete non-growth situation. The *Open Line*, a publication issued by the office of the president of The Christian and Missionary Alliance, reported in its July-August 1982 issue that a persistent problem in the Alliance has been the closing of churches. It has been a significant problem in light of the fact that the ratio in recent years of church closures to new churches established has been approximately thirty percent annually. The district director for church growth of the Pacific Northwest District of The Christian and Missionary Alliance discovered that there were seven prevailing causes of decline. One of the seven causes for decline was weak pastoral leadership. The district then adopted a program whereby the director of church growth worked with the pastor and congregations of the smaller struggling churches to analyze the reasons for decline and then build a long-range strategy for growth. In some cases it meant that congregations needed to recapture their mission and strengthen the leadership.[39] This is just one such case among many that demonstrates so convincingly that growth or non-growth is almost always dependent upon the leadership ingredient.

Across the Atlantic in Britain, Eddie Gibbs reports through an article in the *Global Church Growth Bulletin* that he has identified thirteen growth-arresting diseases which afflict the British churches. One of the thirteen is "leadership tensions" in which he states that eighty percent of local church difficulties are management problems. Other than this one factor of leadership that is a direct cause of growth or non-growth, an analysis of the other twelve "growth-arresting diseases" show that eight of the twelve almost without question have a direct relationship to leadership of the churches.[40] Again it is self-evident that the leadership ingredient is very directly a cause of growth or non-growth.

One of the major reasons that leadership is a cause of non-growth is that leaders too often focus on the internal affairs of the local church. McGavran remarks that we "must recognize that churches have a built-in tendency to be self-centered and ingrown."[41] Charles Chaney in *Design for Church Growth* noted that "In reality, since the late '50s, most American churches have been caught up in the maintenance syndrome."[42] Gibbs in speaking of the growth-arresting diseases of the British churches identifies the "maintenance complex" as the first of thirteen "diseases." In explaining this disease he notes: "Energies are absorbed in keeping the building up and the organizational machinery running." He furthermore states that this "disease" is endemic in Britain.[43] The "maintenance syndrome" is probably the biggest temptation and failure of the Church's leadership. An instinctive human trait is to keep and preserve what we have. In some cases there may be the need to retreat to maintenance in order to reorganize for further advance that will be both qualitative and quantitative. But unfortunately too many Church leaders have retreated to the concern for maintenance and never redirect their efforts to forward advance for the cause of growth. In 1924 John English in *The Minister and His Ministry* most interestingly noted that

> *Perhaps the outstanding weakness of the Christian churches today is that they are more eager to gain converts, to multiply numbers, than they are to train them into a strong, symmetrical, and efficient body.*[44]

Very likely the churches at that time had more concern for church growth than English was willing to accept.

It appears that leaders have the tendency to get burdened down with maintenance of the church. It is not even the question of inner qualitative growth as over against the outer quantitative growth of winning the lost and bringing them into the Church. It is never the question of either quantitative **or** qualitative growth. A truly growing church must never turn away from qualitative to quantitative growth. The Church's leadership must comprehend that qualitative growth would of necessity be concerned that the lost be found and brought to the fold. Donald McGavran boldly points out that it could hardly be considered Christian for the Church to be concerned with qualitative growth and unconcerned with quantitative growth.[45] Thus, a leader with a "church growth conscience"[46] would see maintenance of the church as an effort to bring genuine qualitative growth that would in turn be reflected in quantitative growth. The Church's leadership, a key cause of growth or non-growth of the Church, is responsible to lead the Church in a balanced growth that demonstrates both quality and quantity.

---

[1]Lois McKinney, "Theological Education Overseas: A Church-Centered Approach," paper presented at the 37th annual meeting of the National Association of Evangelicals, Orlando, FL., 6-8 March 1979, p. 1 (Mimeographed).

[2]Donald A. McGavran and Winfield C. Arn, *Ten Steps for Church Growth* (New York: Harper & Row Publishers, 1977), p. 9.

[3]Donald A. McGavran, *Understanding Church Growth* (Grand Rapids: William B. Eerdmans Publishing Company, 1980), p. 41.

[4]Ibid., pp. 43-44.

[5]Ibid., p. 48.

[6]Ibid., pp. 48, 50-51.

[7]McGavran and Arn, *Ten Steps for Church Growth*, pp. 13-14.

[8]Ibid., p. 127.

[9]Ibid., p. 15.

[10]Ibid., p. 16.

[11]Ibid., p. 18.

[12]John Huffman; Larry De Witt; Vernard Eller; John A. Huffman, Jr.; Ben Patterson; and C. Peter Wagner, "Leadership Forum: Must a Healthy Church Be a Growing Church?" *Leadership 2* (Winter 1981):128.

[13]Alan R. Tippett, More than a decade ago, in his classic study, *Solomon Islands Christianity*; and Orlando E. Costas in his report to the Lausanne Congress on World Evangelization, as recorded in *Let the Earth Hear His Voice*, edited by J.D. Douglas; and in Costa's book, *The Church and Its Mission*; have articulated these concepts in more detail.

[14]Charles L. Chaney and Ron S. Lewis, *Design for Church Growth* (Nashville: Broadman, 1977), pp. 6-7.

[15]Ibid., pp. 21-22.

[16]Ibid., p. 7.

[17]McGavran and Arn, *Ten Steps for Church Growth*, p. 21.

[18]Ibid.

[19]Donald McGavran and George G. Hunter III, *Church Growth Strategies that Work* (Nashville: Abingdon, 1980), pp. 25-26.

[20]C. Peter Wagner, *Stop the World I Want to Get On* (Glendale, Calif.: Regal Books, 1974), pp. 75, 77.

[21]Ibid., p. 86.

[22][22]C. Peter Wagner, "Good Pastors Don't Make Churches Grow," *Leadership 2* (Winter 1981):66.

[23]LeRoy Eims, *Be the Leaders You Were Meant to Be* (Wheaton: Victor Books, 1975), p. 7.

[24]John Mahon English, *The Minister and His Ministry* (Philadelphia: The Judson Press, 1924), p. 29.

[25]J. Oswald Sanders, *Spiritual Leadership* (Chicago: Moody Press, 1967), pp. 18-19.

[26]Ibid., p. 19.

[27]E. LeRoy Lawson, *Church Growth: Everybody's Business* (Cincinnati: Standard Publishing, 1975), p. 58.

[28]Delos Miles, *Church Growth — A Mighty River* (Nashville: Broadman Press, 1981), p. 100.

[29]David J. Hesselgrave, *Planting Churches Cross-Culturally: A Guide for Home and Foreign Missions* (Grand Rapids: Baker Book House, 1980), p. 85.

[30]Ibid.

[31]Edward C. Pentecost, *Issues in Missiology: An Introduction* (Grand Rapids: Baker House, 1982), p. 192.

[32]David J. Hesselgrave, ed., *Dynamic Religious Movements* (Grand Rapids: Baker Book House, 1978), p. 299.

[33]Ibid.

[34]Ibid., p. 300.

[35]Ibid., p. 309.

[36]Ibid., p. 299.

[37]Ibid., pp. 301-302.

[38]"Mix" is described as "that combination of ingredients which taken together and in the right proportions produces effective church growth" in McGavran and Arn, *Ten Steps for Church Growth*, p. 129.

[39]The Christian and Missionary Alliance, "New Hope for Dying Churches," *Open Line*, July-August 1982, p. 3.

[40]Eddie Gibbs, "Optimism Spread in British Churches," *Global Church Growth Bulletin* 18 (March-April 1981):96.

[41]McGavran and Arn, *Ten Steps for Church Growth*, p. 20.

[42]Chaney, *Design for Church Growth*, p. 7.

[43]Gibbs, "Optimism Spreads in British Churches," p. 96.

[44]English, *The Minister and His Ministry*, pp. 32-33.

[45]McGavran, *Understanding Church Growth*, p. 425.

[46]"Church growth conscience" is defined as "the conviction that God's will is for the Body of Christ to grow" in McGavran and Arn, *Ten Steps for Church Growth*, p. 127.

CHAPTER II

The Definition Of Leadership In Church Growth

Toward A General Definition Of Leadership

Leadership is recognized as a complex social phenomenon. Men live in social units which have goals around which the unit is structured. Every structured group has a leader or leaders according to that particular structure.[1] This phenomenon exists within a social unit whether the people are playing a game, earning a living, fighting a war, attacking a social evil, or responding to God's love in worship, nurture, and witness. Someone must be engaged in the process of leading if the group is to do anything together.[2]

Men from different backgrounds have defined leadership from their perspectives. From among military leaders, Lord Montgomery defined leadership as the capacity and will to rally men and women to a common purpose which is due to the character of the leader who inspires confidence. Admiral Nimitz defined leadership as that quality in a leader that inspires sufficient confidence in his subordinates as to be willing to accept his views and carry out his commands.[3] President Harry Truman, a political leader, often referred to leaders as people who can get others to do what they do not want to do — and make them like doing it.[4] From the religious realm,

John R. Mott, the noted leader in student circles, defined a leader as a man who knows the road, who can keep ahead, and who pulls others after him.[5]

Leadership is a word that has a wide assortment of meanings. And there are no doubt as many definitions of leadership as there are people to lead. The American Management Association defines leadership as "getting work done through people."[6] This is no doubt the popular definition of leadership. The term leadership can be used to refer to those who occupy the role of a leader. Leadership can also describe a set of functional tasks that must be performed if a group is to carry out its duties.[7] Most frequently, however, leadership is popularly viewed as accomplishing something through people.

The attempt over the years to define leadership in precise terms has yielded a number of theories and definitions. The preoccupation with leadership has occurred predominantly in countries with an Anglo-Saxon heritage. Even though the term did not appear until about the year 1800, there has been no shortage of attempts to define, analyze, and categorize the concept into some tangible entity. Three basic theories of leadership have finally emerged from the thinking of the theorists. Within each basic theory there are numerous studies. The first basic theory sees leadership as traits within the individual leader. The second basic theory sees leadership as a function of the group. The third theory area sees leadership as a function of the situation.[8] The problem with the theorists is that they define leadership from just one dimension. In all actuality leadership involves all three dimensions. It involves certain traits in an individual that make one a leader. Leadership is also clearly a function of a group of people with the function being expedited by the leader for the benefit of the group in a particular situation. The value of the contribution of the theorists is in their detailed thought of each particular dimension.

The three basic theories of leadership that have been put forward do highlight the three dimensions that are clearly evident in leadership. One dimension of leadership involves a consistent set of influencing or serving behaviors that are perceived by others. These are traits in the behavior of a person that cause one to be recognized as a leader. If a person is not perceived as a leader, even though the person wields power or authority, the individual is not a leader. These leadership traits are not only recognized by others but facilitate the process of leading.

Another dimension of leadership is that of performing needed functions of the group. In this dimension leadership serves the needs of the group. It is a task function that contributes to the completion of certain jobs and a relationship function that contributes to smooth human relationships between the people doing the job. Charles Keating in *The Leadership Book* gives some examples of task functions which are:

Initiating	*Any attempt to get an action or movement started. Suggesting a new direction for the group discussion or offering a way to get the discusion going.*
Regulating	*Attempts to order the direction and pace of the group. Calling attention to time, mentioning the agenda, suggesting a structure to go about the task, recalling the group from a tangent.*
Informing	*Giving or soliciting information. Giving opinions, asking opinions, reporting data, asking for data.*
Supporting	*Building on the ideas of another. Supporting another's suggestions or initiations with additional input. Elaborating on the thoughts of another, acknowledging the contributions of another by adding to them.*
Evaluating	*Critiquing the feasibility of an idea. Testing the group of consensus, examining the practicality of a suggestion, helping the group to look at its own process for critique.*
Summarizing	*Digesting the discussion of the group at some point. Sharing with the group what you hear them saying, restating the contributions of another for clarity.*[9]

Keating also gives examples of the relationship functions which are:

Encouraging	*Being friendly, warm, approving.* Telling another you like his or her ideas, smiling or nodding approval, asking another to say more about his or her idea.
Expressing Feelings	*Sharing one's own feelings or the feelings one senses in the group.* Expressing your pleasure in working with the group, pointing out that you feel a tension in the group.
Harmonizing	*Attempts to reconcile disagreements between others.* Getting people to explore their differences, pointing out where you see agreement.
Compromising	*Modifying one's own opinion or feelings for the good of the group.* Admitting error, disciplining oneself to help maintain group cohesion, disciplining oneself to stay at the pace of the group.
Gatekeeping	*Facilitating the participation of others.* Seeking the view of a less vocal participant, suggesting ways that the opinions of all might be expressed, any effort to "open the gate" to fuller use of the group's resources.
Setting Standards	*Expressing norms by which the group may operate.* Offering ground rules for working together, suggesting ways to evaluate the human dynamics of the group, challenging the group to use time or structures better.[10]

The third dimension sees leadership as a function of the situation in which it largely depends upon the needs of others and is even influenced by the needs of the leader. Therefore leadership styles change from group to group and situation to situation. No one leadership style can be considered normative for the style depends upon the needs of a particular situation.[11]

On the basis of these dimensions leadership could be defined as the process in which a person, with recognized qualities of a leader, influences the activities of an individual or group in efforts towards accomplishing goals in a given situation.

Leadership From A Biblical Viewpoint

There is much that can be learned about leadership from Scripture. The Apostle Paul indicated its importance when he told Timothy, "To aspire to leadership is an honourable ambition" (1 Timothy 3:1 NEB). Paul gave Timothy and Titus a leadership responsibility of appointing elders.[12] The salutation in Hebrews 13:24, "Give our greetings to all your leaders and to all God's people" (TEV), is another example which indicates that at the time of the apostles there were leaders and they were recognized as such.[13]

The Bible tells the story of many different kinds of leaders who carry out various programs. There were planners like Joseph and Nehemiah who guided men and women in huge public works projects. An then there were military strategists like Joshua and David who helped form ancient Israel into a nation. There were women who were leaders such as Deborah and Esther who heroically saved their people. Different kinds of men and women of God, all very different in their personalities and powers, became leaders in God's grand program.[14]

The Old Testament, in particular, tells the story of both good and bad leaders. Joseph, Moses, David, and Solomon in his early leadership are examples of good leadership. Eli, Samson, and Saul are examples of men who failed in their leadership roles. The Bible paints a very vivid picture of these leaders without glossing over their errors and problems.[15]

Models of good and bad leadership can be drawn from many of the illustrious characters of the Old Testament. In referring to the Old Testament models Ted Ward makes the very interesting observation that

> These are pre-Christian, some are even pre-scriptural, and they can send us off on the wrong foot. It is alarming how many Christian education textbooks draw an out-of-context model of leadership from Moses.[16]

Of course, as Ward points out, up until the time of Sinai Moses had the Word of God only in oral form. Thus, Moses led God's people through his own adjudication because there was no objective testimony.[17]

The New Testament's concern for leadership is seen as away from momentous events of history. Its attention is given to the spiritual development of the Church. That which is most striking in the New Testament, according to Ted Ward, is the "attunement between the leader and the community."[18] By example and precept Christ taught the disciples about leadership. He was concerned that they learned the spirit of servanthood in preparation for their leadership roles in the early Church.[19] For the most part Jesus rejected the leadership patterns of His day. But for Himself the New Testament is clear that He has all authority and will rule the nations, above all rulers, dominion, and authority. He is Lord and ruler, and in the Church He is the chief shepherd. He has dominion and honor. He commands and gives a new commandment. Thus, consequently obedience is due to Him. These terms that are used in relation to Jesus are avoided for the human relationships in the Church. Where such words of "leadership" or "authority" or "charge" are used the dominant note is that the one so leading should be respected because of what he or she is doing, not for their "office." The person respected is treated so because of the ministry that is carried out in, for, and through the Church. Thus, the leader acts in terms of the needs of the Church.[20]

The ministry of two key New Testament leaders, Peter and Paul, gives a clear view of the leadership style that God desires for His Church. After being taught and trained by Christ and then endued with pentecostal power, Peter became a key leader in the embryonic Church. An example of his leadership style emerged in Acts 6 when the Church is confronted with the needs of the Hebrew and Hellenistic widows. A participatory model of involvement evolves as the apostles turn this matter over to the people. They choose seven leaders who can handle the issue of the widows in a spiritual and competent manner.[21] The important concern of Peter and the deacons chosen by the early Church was for an ongoing ministry in all areas. The leadership, whether that of Peter or of the deacons, was not for the carrying out of authoritative position and power but for equal participation in all phases of ministry.

The Apostle Paul, generally recognized as the greatest leader of the Christian Church, had a leadership style that was essentially counter-cultural for it contradicted first century pagan understandings of leadership.[22] In 1 Thessalonians 2:7-12 Paul describes his relationship to the Thessalonians as a nursing mother, a patient school teacher, and a loving father.[23] Here again the model is that of ministry to the needs of the Church. Paul in no way exerts anything that would reflect position or organizational power but instead that of participating in the needs of believers' lives for the building of the body of Christ.

It is clear that the New Testament does not impose a rigid system of order in the matter of leadership. The universality of the gospel message requires that the Church order serve that universality and permit whatever variety of structures best fosters it in any particular culture.[24] Moreover, the Church can even consciously choose a variety of forms so as to bring the greatest growth possible.

Secular And Christian Views
Of Leadership Compared

In Western cultures leadership is often considered to be inherent in one who is educated for the role or in one who has organizational position. In the Third World leadership is often considered to reside in one who has socio-cultural position and influence or even in one who has gray hair. Jesus reminded His disciples that the Gentiles practiced lordship and not leadership. But He reversed the entire concept of leadership. Jesus demonstrated this by not being domineering, not seeking to profit from His divine position, but cheerfully and eagerly serving those in His care.[25] He articulated His concept of leadership when He said:

> *You know that the rulers of the Gentiles lord it over them, and their great men exercise authority over them. It is not so among you, but whoever wishes to become great among you shall be your servant, and whoever wishes to be first among you shall be your slave; just as the Son of Man did not come to be served, but to serve, and to give His life a ransom for many.[26]*

This is what Jesus considered to be leadership in contrast to the Greco-Roman secular view of prestigious leadership.

Jesus not only rejected the Gentile concept and practice of leadership but in a sense rejected the whole secular leadership style that infected the worship of Jehovah. He had instructed His disciples not be called Rabbi. In Matthew 23:1-12 Jesus refers to what had gone wrong in the synagogues and temples. It was, as Ted Ward expresses it that

> *. . . those who sit in Moses' seat, taking responsibility for the religious leadership of God's people, 1) have made a faulty division between word and deed. They talk a good line but they don't put it into action. 2) They take it upon themselves to tie up neat bundles of tasks for their followers. They see leadership as a matter of deciding what others should do, but they don't actually get down to the hard part themselves. 3) They make their good works highly visible and take their satisfactions from the praises of men. 4) They perpetuate and expand on the traditions of "pomp and circumstance" so as to make*

themselves more distinct from the common people. 5)
They bask in the honors of their rank and accept favors
and privileges as if they were entitled to them. 6) They
like to be called by a distinctive title that represents their
authority and prestige: Rabbi![27]

In the same Matthew passage Jesus even goes a step further
when He instructs the disciples that no one is to call them
Father or even a leader for only God is their Father and Christ
is their leader. The bottom line is, as Jesus says, "But the
greatest among you shall be your servant (Matthew 23:11
NASB). It is clear that relationships are not created by labels
but by relationship-building and that leaders will be recognized
by their servanthood.[28]

All too frequently the concept of leadership within the
Church becomes similar to that of the world. One who is considered a leader is one who holds a high church office or is
the pastor of a large church in an urban center. This is no doubt
due to the common notion of a leader being a great person,
one of attractive personality, a super person, and one of su-
perior abilities. Leadership is thought to be basically an individual achievement.[29] The problem as Kenneth Gangel states
it, is that

> *There are too many attitudes toward leadership preva-*
> *lent even among evangelicals today which have been born,*
> *not of serious commitment to the authority of Scripture,*
> *but rather from the imbibing of society's norms through*
> *a cultural osmosis.*[30]

Gangel identifies and analyzes seven contemporary prevalent
perversions of leadership as found in the Church of the West.
The first is that leaders are born, not made; the second, Christian leadership is ministry from a position of strength and power; the third, human relations serve only as a means to an end;
the fourth, manipulation is acceptable as long as it is geared
toward spiritual goals; the fifth, Christian leadership is

responsible for purifying national politics; the sixth, the authority for Christian leadership resides in the leader; and the seventh, nepotism is a desirable format for leadership transfer.[31]

A simplistic comparison between secular and Christian leadership could be summed up by defining a secular leader as a boss where the Christian leader is a servant. This comparison is epitomized by the following poem:

> *The boss drives his men; the leader coaches them.*
> *The boss depends upon authority; the leader on good will.*
> *The boss says "I"; the leader, "we."*
> *The boss fixes the blame for the breakdown; the leader*
> *   fixes the breakdown.*
> *The boss knows how it is done; the leader shows how.*
> *The boss says "Go"; the leader says "Let's go!"*[32]

Toward A Definition Of Christian Leadership

Christian leadership, to be properly understood, must be defined from the context of the Lordship of Christ. He charactertized the leader as one who serves and whose ministry is redemptive. The motivation of this leadership is love, the method is service, the purpose is redemption,[33] and the result is the glory of God.

The Church is the flock over which Christ rules both directly and through His undershepherds. These undershepherds, as well as those they shepherd, all take orders directly from the Chief Shepherd. Undershepherds are not legislators. Christ as the Chief Shepherd has appointed the undershepherds as leaders and has given to them His authority to lead and manage the flock. This delegated authority is great, yet limited. No authority exists within the Church except that which comes from Christ.[34] Thus, the Christian leader is not a dictator or an employer. Instead he or she is a guide, a member of a team, all of whom are equal in the body of Christ. Christian leadership is essentially a coaching ministry so that every member of the body may work together for growth of the Church. Thus the Christian leader blends the qualities that are both human and divine, a harmonized working of God and the individual, given over to ministry for the growth of the entire body.[35]

After surveying the Biblical data on leadership, Kenneth Gangel has drawn some conclusions regarding the nature of Christian leadership. His five conclusions are as follows:

> 1. Biblical leadership is inseparably linked with identifiable spiritual gifts and a clearcut call from God to distinctive leadership positions.
> 2. Biblical leadership is essentially a servant mentality patterned after the ministry-to-others demonstration of Jesus Himself.
> 3. Biblical leadership places a strong emphasis on the involvement of people and participatory decision-making as opposed to autocracy and authoritarian techniques.
> 4. Biblical leadership always includes the responsibility of teaching and nurturing those whom we lead.
> 5. Biblical leadership requires an attitude of humility and meekness thoroughly demonstrated by Moses and Paul among others, and not to be confused with weakness or indecisiveness.[36]

The next question that emerges concerning Christian leadership is its source from within the Church. Ultimately, as has been discussed, leadership comes from Christ as Lord of the Church. Peter Wagner has suggested that leadership in the body of Christ is acquired in three major ways. The first way is that leadership is earned. The leader earns his/her leadership role by being willing and prepared to serve those whom he/she leads. Love and respect for the leader by the membership of a congregation may of course take time. The second way is that leadership is developed. Leadership training can enhance the ability to lead as long as the person involved senses a commitment to a leadership role. Development of leadership can be carried out in a structured way and as well can be learned over a lifetime. The third way is that leadership is a gift. Training can enhance leadership capabilities but it can only develop a person's abilities to a certain degree. Leadership is one of the spiritual gifts that is given by the Spirit for the building up of the Church.[37]

In relation to the tasks of the Christan leader, James Anderson and Ezra Jones in *The Management of Ministry* have suggested that there are three basic tasks:

> *1. To provide efficient organizational mangement. The brick-and-mortar, bureaucratic aspects of church life demand careful, efficient administration and execution.*
> *2. To provide effective guidance for the gathering church, helping the membership clarify directions and associate together with a free commitment to the mission of the church.*
> *3. To provide authentic spiritual direction — congruent, authoritative teaching, preaching, counsel, and witness in order to help people know themselves and the world through the eyes of faith.*[38]

Each of these tasks has great bearing on the qualitative and quantitative growth of the Church. Where any one of these leadership functions is missing or weak, the Church's ministry and growth will suffer. Anderson and Jones give a model (Figure 1) to show the various functions that are involved in the three basic leadership tasks.

After defining Christian leadership, looking at the source of leadership in the Church, and then defining the basic tasks of the Church's leadership, it is extremely important to examine the kinds of leadership needed for growing churches. Donald McGavran has identified what he calls five classes of leadership which growing churches need. McGavran describes class one leaders as those who serve the existing Church. They are the elders, deacons, board members, Sunday School teachers, choir members, ushers, floral arrangers, and those

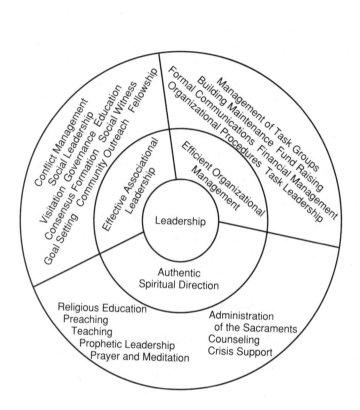

Fig. 1 Model of Parish Leadership Functions[39]

who minister to the sick. These Christians contribute time and energy to the internal ministry of building up the body of Christ. Class one leaders are very important for qualitative growth but their orientation is turned inward and primarily concerned with maintenance of the existing Church. Class two leaders are also volunteer leaders who are turned outward and primarily concerned with outreach. They engage in ministry out from the Church with the goal of bringing people to Christ. They may call upon the unsaved, hold Bible studies or engage in other such activities in order to witness and share the Gospel. Greater numbers of class two leaders are needed in every congregation if the Church is going to experience more dramatic growth. Class three leaders are bivocational leaders who may be paid for part-time ministry. They are leaders of small churches. They have an important role in new churches that are just getting started. Thousands of such leaders are urgently needed by the Church to start new churches, often in small and unimpressive towns and villages around the world. Class four leaders are those who are paid as full-time professional leaders of established churches. These pastors and staff members are important to the ongoing ministry of the Church. Class five leaders are those who work outside or over a number of local churches. They would be men such as district leaders, denominational officials, and mission leaders.[40] These five classes of leaders, as defined by McGavran, are not intended to be a hierarchy of leaders. He is simply defining the kind of leaders that are necessary for a balanced functioning and growth of the Church.[41]

Finally, in defining Christian leadership, it is necessary to realize that the five classes of leaders, who are important for a healthy and growing Church, will have a wide range of leadership styles. The way that leadership is exercised in a particular church, according to Peter Wagner, depends on at least four important factors.

"Cultural ranges" comprise the first factor that influences leadership styles. Within every culture there is a certain range of leadership styles. In many Latin American nations the "strong man" type of leadership is the norm. In Africa and parts of Asia the opposite would be true where the cultural decision-making pattern is by consensus of the group. In England, where the monarchy is a part of life, the Anglican church is ruled by bishops and archbishops. Americans prefer democratic leadership where the vote of the people determines how the leaders function.[42] A leadership style that is culturally relevent is more likely to contribute to a healthy, growing Church.

"Socio-economic ranges" constitute the second factor identified that influences leadership styles. Christian blue-collar workers in America generally expect more directive leadership. Business executives and professionals desire leadership which allows them to be involved in the decision-making process.[43] A leader is much more likely to succeed in church growth efforts if he or she effectively relates to, and takes into account, the sociological and economic situation of his or her particular sphere of ministry.

"Denominational ranges" present the third factor that influences leadership styles. For the Presbyterians the elders and teaching elders work together in the session to lead the church. The Methodists use bishops who have the authority to even remove or assign pastors. The Baptists, however, have a wide range of styles, from strictly congregational governments, to bishop-like pastoral authority in some of the more independent Baptist churches. Thus, each denomination or tradition has developed its own leadership style which determines how their leaders will function.[44] Although denominational traditions are generally quite rigid, the leaders should be willing to adjust their style of leadership if doing so would enhance the growth of their section of the Church.

"Personality ranges" provide the fourth factor that influences leadership styles. Each individual has certain personality traits that determine how he or she will function as a leader. Some leaders are by nature the aggressive, take-charge type whereas for others their style may be more non-directive.[45]

All four factors affect the leadership style of every leader. The Church and its leaders need to be aware of the various factors that influence leadership style so as to consciously maximize the type of style that will contribute to the growth of the Church.

---

[1]Toshihiro Takami, "Concepts of Leadership and Their Meaning for the Growth of Christian Churches" (M.A. thesis, Fuller Theological Seminary, 1969), p. 42.

[2]Arthur Merrichew Adams, *Pastoral Administration* (Philadelphia: The Westminster Press, 1964), p. 14.

[3]Sanders, *Spiritual Leadership*, pp. 31-32.

[4]Charles R. Swindoll, *Hand Me Another Brick* (Nashville: Thomas Nelson Publishers, 1978), p. 16.

[5]Sanders, *Spiritual Leadership*, p. 32.

[6]Ted Ward, "Servants, Leaders and Tyrants," paper presented at Calvin Theological Seminary, Grand Rapids, Mich., 29 March 1978, p. 13. (Mimeographed.)

[7]James D. Anderson and Ezra Earl Jones, *The Management of Ministry* (San Francisco: Harper & Row, 1978), p. 78.

[8]Deanna Ruth Robertson, "A Study of Leadership Style: A Comparison of Secular and Biblical Setting" (M.B.A. thesis, Oral Roberts University, 1980), pp. 10-13. Pp. 10-18 give an excellent but brief summary of the three basic theories of leadership.

[9]Charles J. Keating, *The Leadership Book* (New York: Paulist Press, 1978), p. 14.

[10]Ibid., pp. 13-14.

[11]Ibid, p. 13.

[12]Andrew T. Le Peau, *Paths of Leadership* (Downers Grove: InterVarsity Press, 1983), p. 10.

[13]Ward, "Servants, Leaders, and Tyrants," p. 7.

[14]Le Peau, *Paths of Leadership*, p. 10.

[15]Kenneth Gangel, "Laying a Biblical Foundation," in *Church Leadership Development*, ed. Scripture Press Ministries (Glen Ellyn, Ill.: Scripture Press Ministries, 1977), p. 18.

[16]Ward, "Servants, Leaders, and Tyrants," p. 11.

[17]Ibid., pp. 11-12.

[18]Ibid., p. 12.

[19]Gangel, "Laying a Biblical Foundation," pp. 18-19.

[20]John W. Olley, "Leadership: Some Biblical Perspectives," *The South East Asia Journal of Theology* 18 (No.1-1977):4-6, 10. This is an outstanding detailed exegetical study on the various words that relate to the various aspects of leadership.

[21]Gangel, "Laying a Biblical Foundation," p. 19.

[22]An excellent and concise delineation of various types of first century leadership is given by John W. Olley in his article, "Leadership: Some Biblical Perspectives."

[23]Gangel, "Laying a Biblical Foundation," p. 19.

[24]Olley, "Leadership: Some Biblical Perspectives," p. 17.

[25]A. E. Noorish, *Give Us Men* (Dorset, England: The Overcomer Literature Trust, n.d.), p. 27.

[26]Matthew 20:25-28 (NASB).

[27]Ted Ward, "Facing Educational Issues," in *Church Leadership Development*, ed. Scripture Press Ministries (Glen Ellyn, Ill. Scripture Press Ministries, 1977), p. 44.

[28]Ibid.

[29]Takami, "Concepts of Leadership and Their Meaning for the Growth of Christian Churches," pp. 24, 43.

[30]Gangel, "Laying a Biblical Foundation," p. 20.

[31]Ibid., pp. 20-25.

[32]Lee Lebsack, *Ten at the Top* (Stow, Ohio: New Hope Press, 1974), p. 110.

[33]Richard Wolff, *Man at the Top* (Wheaton: Tyndale House Publishers, 1969), p. 29.

[34]Jay E. Adams, *Pastoral Leadership* (Grand Rapids: Baker Book House, 1975), p. 13.

[35]Sanders, *Spiritual Leadership*, p. 32.

[36]Gangel, "Laying a Biblical Foundation," p. 20.

[37]Wagner, "Good Pastors Don't Make Churches Grow," pp. 69-70.

[38]Anderson and Jones, *The Management of Ministry*, pp. 78-79.

[39]Ibid., p. 80.

[40]Donald A. McGavran and Win C. Arn, *How to Grow A Church* (Glendale, Calif.: Regal Books, 1973), pp. 89-92.

[41]Miles, *Church Growth — A Mighty River*, p. 101.

[42]Wagner, "Good Pastors Don't Make Churches Grow," pp. 67-68.

[43]Ibid., p. 68.

[44]Ibid.

[45]Ibid.

CHAPTER III

The Theology Of Leadership In Church Growth

God Chooses Men And Women To Accomplish His Purposes

"Redemption through a person accents the Biblical conviction that history as a whole must be construed through persons, not through movements or patterns."[1] Groups do not lead, individuals do. A goal, an idea, a vision begins with one person, and then that individual inspires, motivates, and leads a group of people to accomplish it.[2] God is constantly searching for leaders to carry out His purposes, particularly His purposes for the Church. Both the history of Israel and the Church attest to the fact that God is searching for men and women who conform to His highest spiritual requirements. God uses such men and women in leadership roles despite their obvious shortcomings.

A classic example of how God uses men for the accomplishment of His purposes is portrayed in the life of Israel. Deuteronomy 1:9-15 records the history of how the nation had multiplied to the degree that Moses, as a single leader, felt unable to bear the burden alone and settle all disputes. Moses then makes a plea to the people for help: "Choose wise and discerning and experienced men from your tribes, and I will appoint them as your heads" (Deuteronomy 1:13 NASB). Thus, Moses gave the responsibility to the people for the choosing of leaders and then he did the actual appointing. The people accepted this plan for leadership. Deuteronomy 1:15 records the action of Moses appointing heads over the people, leaders of thousands, and of hundreds, of fifties, and of tens. God desires that at every level among His people there are leaders who assist in the carrying out of divine purposes.

"While men are wholly dependent upon the Holy Spirit for the reproduction of life, in paradoxical contrast God has made Himself wholly dependent upon men for the building of His church."[3] Because God is concerned for the growth of the Church, He raises up leadership for His purposes. It is a clear Biblical postulate that God is peculiarly and directly responsible for calling leaders to carry out His purposes. He draws out such individuals for leadership as He wills. He watches over and prepares them. Thus, the ultimate responsibility for Christian leadership belongs to God although the person must act responsibly with God's call to leadership.[4] At this point, A. R. Tippett in his book, *Church Growth and the Word of God*, makes the noteworthy comment that

> The undeniably right idea of God's sovereignty and our obedience can be abused when man is seen as a **mere instrument** in God's hand and not in any way a **responsible agent**.[5]

Paul recognizes a person's position in ministry as a fellow-worker with God (1 Corinthians 3:9; 2 Corinthians 6:1). Thus, a person as God's fellow-worker is held responsible for their ministry. Peter, who was commissioned to feed the lambs and the sheep (John 21:15-17), urged the leaders of the Church to, "shepherd the flock of God among you, not under compulsion, but voluntarily, according to the will of God . . ." (1 Peter 5:2 NASB). Those with this oversight or leadership ministry must realize that they are subject to inspection and appraisal by the Chief Shepherd (1 Peter 5:4).[6] In relation to church growth, this issue is best summed up by Tippett when he says:

> The church growth viewpoint stresses the obedience of man, but it is obedience within a context of responsibility. The human role in this mission to mankind is not mechanical but personal. It implies the existence of special God-given gifts, knowledge of techniques, and responsibility for proficiency . . .
> Certainly he is sovereign, and we should be obedient — that refers to the will. Equally true, we are his co-workers, and therefore we are responsible — that refers to the administration of the techniques and specialized knowledge of our calling. It is to understand this better and to use it more effectively that church growth research has been established.[7]

Christ Trains Individuals To Build His Church

Men were Christ's method for the accomplishment of His work. His evangelistic strategy was to use men to take the Gospel. Christ did not design special kinds of programs to reach the multitudes. He in turn put his emphasis upon training men who would minister to the people. Christ recruited these men before He launched an evangelistic campaign or preached a sermon in public. Christ's initial objective was to recruit and train men who could lead in carrying on His work after He returned to the Father.[8] Jesus has stated in no uncertain terms that He would build His Church. When he departed into heaven he left the task of building the Church to the members of His body. While all members of the body participate in the building of the Church, Paul makes it very clear that there are leaders, namely, apostles and prophets, who have a unique ministry in that building process. These apostles and prophets are referred to as the foundation of the Church which is a clear indication of their unique role as leaders (Ephesians 2:19-20).

The genius of Jesus' strategy was that although He would do what He could do to help the multitudes, He would devote Himself primarily to a few men. His disciples, the early leaders of the Church, were the vanguard of His developing movement. Men were so important to His program that prior to the selection of the disciples He spent all night in prayer (Luke 6:12-16). When the disciples were chosen there was no indication that they had the potential to become leaders. But they had a willingness to follow and learn. Christ spent a great amount of his time and energy in training these men.[9] Robert Coleman in his book, *The Master Plan of Evangelism*, lays out eight principles that Jesus used to train His disciples to become leaders. They were:

1. Selection   Men were His method.
2. Association   He stayed with them.
3. Consecration   He required obedience.
4. Impartation   He gave Himself away.
5. Demonstration   He showed them how to live.
6. Delegation   He assigned them work.
7. Supervision   He kept check on them.
8. Reproduction   He expected them to reproduce.[10]

Jesus' emphasis upon the training of the few, rather than upon a wide ministry to the multitudes, clearly reflects His deep concern for those men who would be the leaders in establishment and growth of His Church. Jesus had given His life to bring the Church into being, and He expects His leaders to give their lives for the growth and development of that Church. The Apostle Paul, following the example of the Master, likewise concentrated on potential leaders such as Timothy, John Mark, Aquilla and Priscilla, Philemon, and others.[11]

Holy Spirit Ordains And Equips Individuals For Leadership Ministry

Throughout history the Holy Spirit has chosen to ordain and equip individuals for leadership roles in the Church.

Through the centuries there have been literally thousands of unknown men and women who have led the Church in a dynamic growth pattern through the help of the Holy Spirit.[12] It is not greatness of the human endeavor, or the amount of work accomplished that produces successful ministry and brings growth to the Church. It is the prerogative and ministry of the Holy Spirit to use known and unknown leaders for the cause of church growth. The role of the Holy Spirit in relation to human efforts is well articulated by Terry Young in his article, "The Holy Spirit and the Birth of Churches":

> *The Holy Spirit chooses to work through the human efforts that we put forth, and the more vigorous and varied our efforts, the better the opportunity that the Holy Spirit has to do his work of producing a spiritual harvest. Our busyness does not guarantee the presence and work of the Holy Spirit. Our efforts only furnish him the opportunity to work. Properly understood, the church is absolutely dependent upon the work of the Spirit for any effectiveness in its efforts to reach men for Christ.*[13]

When Christ commissioned His disciples to be leaders in His Church He gave the Holy Spirit to the disciples as their guide (John 20:22). When the earthly Jesus is no longer on earth He is represented by the Spirit. The letters to the churches, dictated by the exalted Christ, repeat seven times, ". . . hear what the Spirit says to the churches" (Revelation 2:7, 11, 17, 29; 3:6, 13, 22). Christ speaks to the Church through the Spirit, and until the Second Coming the Spirit is Christ's representative on earth. Thus, Christ rules His Church through the Spirit. In relation to the ministry of the Holy Spirit in the leadership of the Church, Rudolf Bohren in *Preaching and Community* makes some very perceptive comments:

> *There is therefore no legitimate leadership of the congregation apart from the Spirit. There can be no act of leadership that takes place without the Spirit. All leadership within the congregation must therefore be*

57

*interrogated to see whether it is leadership in the Spirit,
leadership itself led by the Spirit. The question of leadership is ultimately a question of the presence of Christ in
the congregation, a question of the working of the Spirit.
It is therefore not primarily technical, but theological,
a question of faith, that is, of obedience in faith. The
leadership of the congregation is not something that can
be established once and for all; it must accept the right
of the congregation continually to ask whether it is proper
leadership. It is the duty of the congregation to test spirits
(1 John 4:1). Even and especially the spirit of leadership!*[14]

The Holy Spirit gives gifts that are essential for church growth. Peter Wagner, in his book *Your Spiritual Gifts Can Help Your Church Grow*, laments the fact that books on spiritual gifts do not relate the gifts directly and specifically to the growth of the Church. He notes the fact that most sources explain "how the gifts help individual believers, how they bring about maturity in the Church in general, and how they enhance Christian unity and brotherhood."[15] Thus, according to Wagner, the gifts must be seen "not as ends in themselves, but as means toward an end."[16]

One of the extremely important means for achieving church growth is through Spirit-gifted leadership. The New Testament shows that Christian leadership is developed by the Holy Spirit. He ordains or calls individuals into certain leadership roles within the Church. He then provides the spiritual gifts as equipment for special leadership roles.[17] The Holy Spirit equips this leadership so that they can guide every believer in discovering, developing and deploying his or her gifts in ways that contribute to the growth of the entire body of Christ.[18]

In relation to the gifts there needs to be a distinction between "ministry functions" and "leadership functions."[19] All believers equipped with spiritual gifts can and should have a ministry in and outside the Church. There are certain believers who are obviously equipped with specific spiritual gifts that may cast them in a leadership function of the Church. In relation to these functions Peter Wagner has said that "When the two are properly distinguished, strong Church leadership can be maintained, avoiding at the same time the ever-present danger of clericalism."[20] All believers have a ministry function but not necessarily a leadership function. Those who have a leadership ministry may have such a function because they have been gifted with a spiritual gift such as mentioned in Ephesians 4:11. The spiritual gifts of apostle, prophet, evangelist, pastor, and teacher inherently cast one into at least an unofficial leadership capacity, if not official in many cases.

Leslie Flynn points out in his book, *19 Gifts of the Spirit*, that there may be those who have the gift of shepherding or teaching or ruling but who may not hold an official office in that capacity.[21] The matter of holding the Church's organization is immaterial to the issue. A person can hold an office and yet not lead. A believer can lead through certain spiritual gifts whether or not he or she is holder of an official office. Thus, the leadership function can be broken down into two divisions. There are those who lead through an office in the church's organization. Their leadership in this capacity should be geared so as to bring growth to the Church. There are those who give leadership to the Church through the exercise of gifts, particularly the gifts mentioned in Ephesians 4:11, sometimes holding an office in the Church, sometimes not. It is absolutely obligatory that these kind of leaders carry out their ministry in such a way that it contributes significantly to quality and quantity church growth.

Conclusion — The Divine Design For Church Growth Through Human Leadership

There is no question that God is at work in the world establishing His Church. The basic problem of the Church is cooperating with the divine plan to further its growth. The great Biblical disclosure is that men and women are to participate in the work of God. Hollis Green points out that Luke's writings show him to be preoccupied with the human element and how that human element fits into God's design. Green contends that Luke's theology cannot be understood until his concern for the human element is discovered and understood as a frame of reference for his writings. This perspective is shown primarily in his selection of parables and incidents he chooses to relate from the life and teaching of Jesus.[22] Michael Green has carefully researched the evangelism program of the early Church. He also focuses upon the important role that the early believers and their leaders had in the expansion of the Church by devoting one entire chapter to the human element that was involved in the growth of the early Church.[23] It is clear that God's design for His work on earth is for it to be accomplished through the human element. Not only was God's redemption carried out through a man, but the ongoing program of the Church in the world today is carried out through individual persons.[24]

If a person is vitally involved in the divine program to build the Church, it means that a great responsibility rests upon the leadership of the Church. Church leaders cannot escape by using God's sovereignty as the reason for poor church growth. They cannot blame God for wood, hay and stubble. Leaders will be held responsible for the quality of their work directed toward church growth. Michael Griffiths sums up the issue well in his book, *The Church & World Mission*:

> It seems then that we Christians must accept responsibility for the state of the churches and the progress of mission, and that we cannot, biblically, blame God for either. We must not allow an overstress on the antitheses between church and kingdom, divine sovereignty and human responsibility or the **missio Dei** and the **missio ecclesiae** to excuse our burying our heads in the sand. The kingdom is the reign of God and he is sovereign. But the church is the gathering (**Sammlung**) and sending (**Sendung**) of men and we are responsible for it before God, because he himself chooses to make us so.[25]

---

[1]Wolff, *Man at the Top*, p. 3.

[2]Paul W. Powell, *How to Make Your Church Hum* (Nashville: Broadman Press, 1977), p. 32.

[3]Vergil Gerber, "Starting and Organizing Local Churches Overseas," *Evangelical Missions Quarterly* 6 (Fall 1969):30.

[4]P. T. Chandapilla, "How to Develop Indian Leaders," *Evangelical Missions Quarterly* 5 (Spring 1969):152-53.

[5]A. R. Tippett, *Church Growth and the Word of God* (William B. Eerdmans Publishing Company, 1970), p. 18.

[6]Ibid., pp. 18-19.

[7]Ibid., p. 19.

[8]Robert E. Coleman, "The Master's Plan," in *Perspectives on the World Christian Movement*, ed. Ralph D. Winter and Steven C. Hawthorne (Pasadena: William Carey Library, 1981), p. 71.

[9]Gerber, "Starting and Organizing Local Churches Overseas," p. 36.

[10]Robert E. Coleman, *The Master Plan of Evangelism* (Old Tappen, N.J.: Fleming H. Revell Company, 1972), p. 7.

[11]Gerber, "Starting and Organizing Local Churches Overseas," p. 36.

[12]Lawson, *Church Growth: Everybody's Business*, pp. 57-58.

[13]Terry J. Young, "The Holy Spirit and the Birth of Churches," in *The Birth of Churches*, ed. Talmadge R. Amberson (Nashville: Broadman, 1979), p. 172.

[14]Rudolf Bohren, *Preaching and Community* (Richmond, Va.: John Knox Press, 1965), pp. 195-96.

[15]C. Peter Wagner, *Your Spiritual Gifts Can Help Your Church Grow* (Glendale, Calif.: Regal Books, 1974), p. 11.

[16]Ibid.

[17]Chandapilla, "How to Develop Indian Leaders," p. 152.

[18]Adams, *Pastoral Leadership*, p. 13.

[19]Wagner, "Good Pastors Don't Make Churches Grow," pp. 68, 71.

[20]Ibid., p. 71.

[21]Leslie B. Flynn, *19 Gifts of the Spirit* (Wheaton: Victor Books, 1974), p. 24.

[22]Hollis L. Green, *Why Churches Die: A Guide to Basic Evangelism and Church Growth* (Minneapolis: Bethany Fellowship, 1962), pp. 7-8.

[23]Michael Green, *Evangelism in the Early Church* (Grand Rapids: William B. Eerdmans Publishing Company, 1970), pp. 166-93.

[24]Quentin Lockwood, "The Growth of Churches," in *The Birth of Churches*, ed. Talmadge R. Amberson (Nashville: Broadman, 1979), p. 154.

[25]Michael Griffiths, *The Church & World Mission* (Grand Rapids: Zondervan Publishing House, 1980), pp. 21-22.

CHAPTER IV

The History Of Leadership In Church Growth

Leadership — Key Component In Growth Of Religious Movements

The important function of leadership in the growth of the Christian Church around the world is a phenomenon that is not unique to the Christian religion. Leadership is also an important factor in the growth of other religious movements. David Hesselgrave's book, *Dynamic Religious Movements*, gives an account of a number of twentieth century religious movements that have experienced rapid growth and expansion. In analyzing the key components that contributed to the tremendous growth of these movements, Hesselgrave notes that special leadership was most significant. These fast growing movements had outstanding leadership, most of whom were somewhat charismatic. One feature of their leadership was that they exhibited a deep sense of call and mission. Even though the leaders of these movements were very different from each other, it is clear from their record that they were effective leaders in their own religious and cultural contexts. Hesselgrave notes that these leaders had "an overwhelming sense of call and mission, the insistence upon divine authority, an unusual capacity for sacrifice and work, the ability to communicate."[1]

Case Studies Portray Leadership As A Key Factor In Church Growth

Leadership in Local Churches

In analyzing growing congregations it does not take long to see that one of the key factors that influences the growth is the Church's leadership. Generally the leader who influences the growth most significantly is the pastor. Elmer Towns has written a book on growing churches, *Getting a Church Started in the Face of Insurmountable Odds with Limited Resources in Unlikely Circumstances*, the title of which accurately describes the contents of his book. In church after church, as Towns tells the story, one of the key factors that contributed to the starting of a congregation against all odds was the leadership of the pastor. In a young Milwaukee congregation the pastor told the people that God uses a leader in every congregation. This pastor intended to be that kind of man. He observed that the stable, conservative people of Milwaukee responded more to a strong pastor than to a committee. The result was that this congregation experienced fantastic growth. In telling the story of a church in Salem, Virginia, Towns observes that the unbelievable growth of the congregation is a story of a young man with an indomitable will.[2]

Tom Minnery was commissioned by the editors of *Leadership* to evaluate and analyze three congregations that were thoroughly different in methods, setting, and philosophy, yet all showing unique marks of achievement. After researching all three congregations Minnery observes that

> *the main thing that became apparent was that God works in great diversity. I found no "secret of the successful church," but instead, strains of similarity interrupted by chunks of contradiction.*[3]

However, in spite of the diversity Minnery found one common dynamic in each of the churches. That one dynamic was a pastor who believed he knew what the Lord wanted of him and consequently tried to follow that leading.[4] One of the requirements of the author's church growth class at Toccoa Falls College each semester was to have every student do a church growth analysis[5] on a local congregation. These surveys affirmed, in most cases, that the pastor was the key factor or one of the important factors in a growth situation, lack of growth or even in non-growth.

Unusual growth has also been experienced in congregations of the Third World. In Singapore, Trinity Christian Church of the Assemblies of God started in a pastor's home in 1969 with only ten persons. By 1981 the membership had reached 608 and the Sunday School attendance had arisen to 1,500. The assistant pastor said that there were six factors that were the secret of their growth. Two of the six factors relate to leadership. The very first factor cited was strong and dynamic leadership and the other factor, the fifth one, was aggressive, motivated departmental leaders.[6]

Another example comes from Latin America. Pastor Bruno Radzisewski in Rosario, Argentina, had been very discouraged and was deeply frustrated in his small struggling church. But at the point of resignation Pastor Bruno found some answers which contributed to a mangnificent growth pattern in his church. In an eighteen month period his faithful few zoomed from thirty-five regular attenders to more than 150! So, instead of receiving denominational subsidy, the congregation began paying a tithe to the district. The old building was replaced, the parsonage was repaired, and Sunday School rooms were added. The key to this transformation was that Pastor Bruno attended a church growth seminar which launched him into a plan that would dramatically change his ministry and his church. Out of the seminar Pastor Bruno developed a plan of developing house churches through prayer cells led by laymen who were carefully trained for the task. It was simply the centuries-old pattern of equipping the saints for the work of the ministry.[7] While the plan is certainly sound, the key factor behind the success of the plan and the growth of the congregation was the fact that a man, Pastor Bruno, began to provide aggressive leadership and enlisted others to also take leadership roles.

Pastors often admit that growth, or even the lack of it, has a direct relationship to themselves and their ministries. A pastor in Staten Island, New York, ministered in a church for nine years with an increase from sixteen to barely a hundred. But this pastor, after getting a hold on church growth principles, began acting upon them to see aggressive growth. The church grew from 200 to 700 members in little more than four years.[8] This all happened after an aggressive pastor led the church with sound church growth principles. A pastor in Trenton, Michigan, was exposed to a church growth seminar and felt that it was the greatest thing since Pentecost. It not only affected him as a pastor, but he began training the leadership of the congregation. In addition he opened the board meetings with church growth discussion. As a result seventy-six percent of the membership is actively engaged in congregational activity over and above worship services and Bible study. Attendance jumped from 350 in 1974 to an average of 930 in 1981. About 900 out of the 1,200 members are involved in one of the twenty-seven home Bible study groups. Again growth came because a man, the pastor, became aware of and excited about church growth, and then led the other leaders of the congregation in the direction of "soul-winning and soul-keeping."[9]

Quentin Lockwood in his article, *The Growth of Churches*, analyzed two churches in a large Midwestern city. Both churches were started about the same time in an area on the edge of the city where the communities were extremely similar. One began growing immediately as the congregation met in temporary quarters. The other congregation grew more slowly, giving much time and attention to property and construction of a temporary facility. The first group grew to 700 members, baptizing about fifty people per year. The other group grew to less than one hundred members and baptized less than ten people per year. Lockwood advances several reasons for the difference in growth rate. The growing church had only one pastor who preached a Christ-centered message with an emphasis on personal evangelism. The church also placed an emphasis on growing from the very beginning and quickly moved to indigenous leadership with a focus on people and not on facilities. The other congregation had short-term pastors, spent much time on getting facilities, and its leadership continued to be transplanted members from other areas. Finally the congregation met its demise and the property was sold.[10] Again this is a classic example in which the congregation that puts emphasis on leaders and people experiences growth. The congregation that ignores the important aspect of stable leadership, and emphasizes property and buildings, will likely experience its demise.

Leadership In Groups Of Churches

O.D. Emery in his book, *Concepts to Grow By*, looks at the growth patterns of fifty local churches of all sizes. In analyzing what makes a church grow Emery notes that there are three basic areas of strength that are common in growth situations. They are attitudes, leadership, and outreach. In relation to attitudes Emery notes that a growth conscience is necessary for growth. In relation to outreach Emery points out that the growth conscience should produce an outreach program at all costs. In looking at fifty different churches Emery clearly articulates what is needed in the way of leadership so that a congregation can grow:

> *Growing churches are movements which have purposeful leadership. Some of this leadership must generally be found in the pastor. Often the leadership is distributed among several persons who have the spark that ignites men to follow their cause. All growing churches have strong leaders. These leaders are not always*

*persons holding office in the congregation, but they are
people of vision and determination who have a sense of
what God wants done and are restless to get at it. In any
growing local church a degree of momentum is discerni-
ble within the spirits of many or at least a few. This becomes the leadership potential for what God has in mind
to accomplish. As that leadership nucleus seeks to know
what God intends for their congregation, they find themselves extended in vision, humbled by spiritual discipline,
and sacrificed to serve as stimuli for the entire congregational body.*[11]

The 188th General Assembly (1976) Report on United Pres-
byterian Church Membership Trends identified the pastor as
the key to church growth. The report points out that the pastor must be well prepared, deeply committed, hard-working,
clear in vision, and capable of arousing enthusiasm in the congregation. In commenting on church growth in mainline congregations, Carl Dudley in his book, *Where Have All Our
People Gone?* says that

*effective pastors are not passive in their leadership.
. . . They provide good leadership, not as a stellar activity,
but as a faithful servant in the whole community.*[12]

Paul Orjala in his book, *Get Ready to Grow: A Strategy
for Local Church Growth*, gives an account of a 1977 survey
that examined the church growth in fast growing Nazarene
churches. The survey identified factors accounting for growth
in their ministry and evangelism. The top four characteristics
were

*(1)A shepherd-type pastoral ministry; (2) A pastor who
had good personal relationships in the church and community; (3) A pastor who was supported by a church
membership that also had good personal relations among
themselves and in their community; and (4) A pastor and
members who were effective in developing need-centered
outreach ministries.*[13]

The pastor must want the congregation to grow and be willing to pay the price for it. Such a pastor believes that God wants his congregation to grow and works with that end in mind.

An analysis was made of 425 of the fastest growing churches in the Southern Baptist Convention. Seven key factors were identified as the vital signs of the growth in these churches. The first factor of the seven was pastoral leadership. The pastor was the kind of man who was a possibility thinker and whose dynamic leadership had been used to catalyze the entire church into action for growth.[14]

In many areas around the world Church leadership is making a most unique contribution to church growth. In Asia, for example, this is the case. In the Philippines the Alliance Church (CAMACOP) had significant growth during the period between 1948 and 1952. During those years the baptized members increased from 4,339 to 10,093. At the same time the number of national pastors and missionaries almost doubled. It has been noted that during this period there were strong, dedicated national and missionary leaders. In addition lay preachers were systematically trained.[15] In Korea the pastor has been identified to be of primary importance in the growth and development of the Church.[16] It has been pointed out that the pastors in Korea set an example. They practice personal evangelism and they train their people to do the same. They do not just tell their people to do it but train the people how to do it.[17]

Lessons Learned From Leadership's Involvement In Church Growth

It is not just in the last several decades that leadership has played such a major role in church growth, or something that has just been articulated by the Church Growth Movement. Leadership always played a major role in the growth and establishment of the Church around the world, even prior to the present day thinking on church growth.

In the early days of the Church's expansion the Gospel was spontaneously spread by informal evangelists. Every Christian felt called to be a witness to Christ in word and deed. Each believer was in a sense an apologist, at least to the extent of being ready to give a good account of the hope that was within them.[18] In addition to all Christians who engaged in witness there were those leaders who had a key role in extending the boundaries of the Church. Thus, there were those such as Paul, Barnabas, Timothy, and others, who were set apart by the Church for a particular leadership role. Paul in turn trained other leaders who in turn became church planters in various places.[19]

Church histories are often concerned with such things as church doctrine, ecclesiastical machinery, church feuds, Papal bulls, religious wars, church councils and other such things. But from another perspective church history is an account of how God used many different kinds of persons, with varied leadership styles, to lead the Church in its expansion. K.S. Latourette, in his seven volumes[20] of church history, gives a thorough treatment of hundreds of Church leaders who played a significant role in leading the Church in its growth. In looking at the Church's history from the angle of leadership and church growth, it is clear that one prominent factor in the growth of the Church was the role of leaders who were used by God to accomplish great results in evangelism and church planting.

Just a few examples illustrate the role of key leaders in the establishment and growth of the Church. Although others may have participated in the establishment of the Church in Armenia, Gregory the Illuminator is considered the founder. In Ireland Patrick gets the credit for the founding of the Church. Ludwig Nommensen dominated the birth of the Christian Church among the Bataks in Indonesia.[21] Adoniram Judson established churches in Burma. John Wesley established churches throughout England.[22]

Growing churches do not develop out of community consensus or committee effort. Both from Scripture and history it is evident that growing churches have aggressive pastors.[23] Peter Wagner has observed that especially in America the pastor is the primary catalytic factor for growth in the local church. It may not always be the case in other countries where churches are multiplying much more rapidly than pastors can be trained and ordained.[24] If it is not the pastor it is rare that significant church growth comes spontaneously without some strong personality who provides dynamic leadership and coordination. The important thing is that there is an individual, whether it be pastor or not, who serves as the catalyst or the strong figure around whom the others can rally for the cause of church growth.[25]

---

[1]Hesselgrave, *Dynamic Religious Movements*, pp. 309-10.

[2]Elmer L. Towns, *Getting a Church Started in the Face of Insurmountable Odds with Limited Resources in Unlikely Circumstances* (Nashville: Impact Books, 1975), pp. 25, 56, 70.

[3]Thomas A. Minnery, "Success in Three Churches: Diversity and Originality," *Leadership* 2 (Winter 1981):57, 65.

[4]Ibid., p. 65.

[5]For this analysis the students used Bob Wagmire and C. Peter Wagner, *The Church Growth Survey Handbook*. 2nd ed. (Santa Clara, Calif.: The Global Church Growth Bulletin, 1980).

[6]Alfred C. H. Yeo, "Singapore's Secret of Success," *Asia Theological News*, July-September 1982, pp. 18-19.

[7]Juan Carlos Miranda, " 'Rosario' Came Just In Time," *Church Growth Bulletin* 14 (September 1977):150-51.

[8]Daniel Mercaldo, Frederick J. Finks, and Wayne A. Pohl, "Growth Around the World: Growing Churches in the U.S.A." *Global Church Growth Bulletin* 18 (September-October 1981):139.

[9]Ibid., p. 140.

[10]Lockwood, "The Growth of Churches," p. 156.

[11]O. D. Emery, *Concepts to Grow By* (Marion, Ind.: The Wesley Press, 1976), 9-10, 50.

[12]Carl S. Dudley, *Where Have All Our People Gone?* (New York: The Pilgrim Press, 1979), pp. 105-114.

[13]Paul R. Orjala, *Get Ready to Grow: A Strategy for Local Church Growth* (Kansas City: Beacon Hill Press of Kansas City, 1978), p. 96.

[14]Donald E. Riggs, *Make It Happen* (Warsaw, Ind: LP Publications, 1981), p. 44.

[15]David Lloyd Rambo, "Training Competent Leaders for the Christian and Missionary Alliance Churches of the Philippines" (M.A. thesis, Fuller Theological Seminary, 1969), pp. 63, 65.

[16]Marlin L. Nelson, "Korea: Asia's First Christian Nation?" *Asia Theological News* 8 (July-September 1982):14.

[17]Bong Rin Ro, ed. "Crisis in the Local Church," *Asia Theological News* 8 (July-September 1982):2.

[18]Green, *Evangelism in the Early Church*, p. 175.

[19]Stephen Neill, *A History of Christian Missions* (Baltimore: Penguin Books, 1964), pp. 22-24.

[20]Kenneth Scott Latourette, *A History of the Expansion of Christianity*, 7 vols. (New York: Harper & Brothers, 1937-1945).

[21]Harold R. Cook, *Historic Patterns of Church Growth* (Chicago: Moody Press, 1971), p. 106.

[22]Towns, *Getting a Church Started in the Face of Insurmountable Odds with Limited Resources in Unlikely Circumstances*, p. 170.

[23]Ibid., pp. 170-75.

[24]C. Peter Wagner, *Your Church Can Grow* (Glendale, Calif.: Regal Books, 1976), p. 55.

[25]Cook, *Historic Patterns of Church Growth*, p. 106.

CHAPTER V

The Preparation Of Leadership In Church Growth

The need of trained leadership for the well-being and growth of the people of God is not a contemporary issue. Schools of the prophets were established and led by Samuel. During the days of Elijah and Elisha, schools of the prophets were established at Gilgal, Bethel, and other cities. Richard Wolff has noted that

> As a result, from the days of Solomon to the very last days of the kindgom of Judah, there always was an adequate supply of men to fill the ranks of official prophets . . . . By way of contrast it is important to notice that before the call of Samuel, who established such schools, the prophetic word was rare in Israel and prophecy was not widespread.[1]

Need Of Trained Leadership For Growing Churches

The growth of the Church around the world is a cause for rejoicing, but it is also a cause for deep concern. As the number of believers is increasing and new churches are being planted every day, the need for church leaders increases.[2] Trained leaders are urgently needed. Bong Rin Ro, in an article about the Church in Asia, observes that in some places the reason the Church is "not growing is because they lack well-trained top leadership."[3] In another article Bong Ro, one of the outstanding Christian leaders in Asia, refers to the fact that there are some 500 theological schools in Asia, ranging from tribal Bible schools to graduate seminaries. But Ro observed that most Christians in Asia do not realize the importance of advanced training for local church leaders in the growth of the Church. According to Ro, this problem is one of seven important issues of Asian Theological Education. It is noteworthy that this concern for theological education, as it relates to church growth, is the first issue that Ro lists among the seven.[4] In Africa the same problem exists. SIM International has warned that there will be spiritual disaster unless pastoral training can keep pace with the present high growth rate. The SIM-related congregations in Africa have doubled every ten years since 1945. In 1945 there were 500 churches and by 1975 there were more than 4,000.[5]

It is clear that God always has a plan to raise up trained leadership for the growth of His people. This is evidenced in the ministry of Christ who devoted a great deal of attention to training His disciples. Wolff notes that

> *According to the Gospel of Mark, at least three distinct moments Jesus isolated Himself with the twelve for more specific indoctrination and training. Leadership is part of the Biblical pattern.*[6]

Trained leadership always has been and always will be an important need in God's program. Trained leadership is an integral part of the quantitative and qualitative growth of God's people. James Wong in his article, "Training of the Ministry for Rapid Church Growth," contends that the bottom line of leadership or theological training is church growth. He makes the following clear statement on the issue:

*Matters of curriculum, entrance requirements, length
of course, level of study, academic accreditation etc. can
be resolved only in the light of the larger issue of purpose and function. I submit that if our institutions and
seminaries — be they extension or residential — do not
produce men and women who are concerned for Church
growth and equipped to plant new Churches in responsive areas our program of theological education has failed
in its job. Theological degrees, academic excellence, post-
graduate scholarship and many other issues must not be
regarded as the goal and purpose of theological education. Our chief and fundamental concern — whether as
pastors, evangelists or theological educators — should
be the obedient carrying out of the Great Commission
and effecting the rapid multiplication of new congregations.[7]*

When the need of trained leadership is not viewed from
the perspective of church growth, the Church will busy itself
with training leadership for maintaining the existing Church,
particularly its organization. The result is Church leaders who
are academic scholars and management experts instead of
church growth practitioners. This kind of leader is reduced to
an "organizational man" in a gray flannel clerical garb. Such
leaders most unfortunately are functionaries rather than men
of vision for the growth of the Church.[8] There is a need for
trained leadership in the Church but it must be the right kind
of training in order to produce the right kind of leader. In the
planning for the training of the ministry, Lois McKinney has
put forward four important assumptions that undergird our
planning:

*(1) Trained leaders are essential to the growth of the
church; (2) effective training for leaders must be systematically planned and executed; (3) plans for leadership
training are determined by (a) the **kinds** (or categories)
of leaders churches need and (b) the **number** of leaders
churches need; and (4) plans for leadership training must*

*be based on accurate appraisals of **present** leadership needs, and realistic projections of **future** leadership needs.*[9]

It is most significant that the first assumption is that growth of the Church depends upon trained leaders. If the entire Church of Jesus Christ would work from this basic assumption there would certainly be greater growth in the Church than we are seeing today. This assumption would revolutionize theological education away from an orientation of training for the maintenance of the Church to an orientation of both maintenance and growth, in proper perspective and balance, so that the Church can truly grow in every dimension.

Type Of Trained Leadership Needed
For Growing Churches

The Church must ask itself what type of leadership furthers the cause of Christ, honors the name of Christ, and furthers the Church of Christ. From the perspective of the types of leaders that needed theological education, Lois McKinney has identified five categories which are:

Level 1: local leaders. Local leaders are the persons who exercise teaching, preaching, administrative, and evangelistic functions within a local congregation.

Level 2: overseers of small congregations. Overseers of small congregations are those who hold a small congregation together or share in the direction of a larger congregation.

Level 3: overseers of a large congregation or of clusters of small congregations. Overseers of a large congregation or of clusters of small congregations often function as circuit-riding ministers to scattered groups of believers. In some cases, particularly in urban areas, they may lead one large congregation rather than several small ones.

*Level 4: regional, national, and international adminis-
trators. Regional, national, and international adminis-
trators are the persons who tie associations of churches
together.*

*Level 5: educator-scholars. Educator-scholars are
specialists who exercise their influence upon the church
through scholarly research and the development of theological disciplines.*[10]

McKinney's categories of leadership are an adaptation of
McGavran's five levels of leadership.[11] McKinney's level one
leaders are a combination of McGavran's level one leaders,
unpaid leaders within local congregations who serve and maintain the Church, and level two leaders, unpaid leaders within
local congregations who reach out through witnessing and
evangelism. By combining McGavran's level one and level two
leaders, McKinney has added her level five leaders because of
its relevance to the concerns of theological education.
McGavran's perspective on the types of leaders needed by the
Church is from the concern for church growth. McKinney's
perspective as to the types of leaders the Church needs is from
the angle of those who need theological education. In order
to accommodate both perspectives it is suggested that
McGavran's levels one and two be kept separate in order to
maintain the distinction of leaders who are engaged in direct
evangelistic church growth efforts. Thus, in addition to the
five levels suggested by McGavran, a sixth level would be added to incorporate McKinney's fifth level leader who is an edu-
cator and scholar. Even this level of Church leadership should
have a perspective in their type of ministry that ultimately contributes to church growth. All six levels of leaders are equally
important to the Church. Each level of leader urgently needs
the type of training that is appropriate for its level — most
of all so their respective ministries will directly or ultimately
bring growth to the Church in every dimension.

The real issue for the Church may not be so much the types of leadership needed. The real issues are two-fold. First, the Church needs the proper balance of all six levels of leadership. So it is a question of how many leaders in each level the Church trains for the maximum rate of growth. The Church must constantly assess the ratio of each level of leadership needed so as to attain the maximum church growth. The second issue is that of the educational process and whether or not it trains leaders to have a church growth conscience. Dealing with these two issues with appropriate answers will enable the concerns for Church members and Church leaders to be merged into a common effort to build up the Church of Jesus Christ.

In terms of basic skills, the type of leadership needed in the Church is that which is trained for winning people to Christ, building up believers in the use of their gifts, and planting churches. Norman Shawchuck, writing in *Christianity Today*, states the problem as follows:

> *Theological education has equipped leaders to be mechanics — that is, to do what's needed to keep the machine running. But church leaders today must be architects, not mechanics; managers and shapers of the future, not precedent followers of the past.*[12]

Christ called and trained his disciples to be fishers of men. The disciples were to be expectant of a harvest (John 4:35-38). It is to be an abundant harvest; so many laborers are needed (Matthew 9:37-38). Christ trained his men in order that there would be visible results. However, the type of leader being trained today tends to have a totally academic orientation. At least a few theological institutions are trying to produce the right type of leadership although their approach may be considered rather revolutionary by most. The Evangelical Theological Seminary of Indonesia is attempting to maintain a balance between the practical and the academic by requiring every student to plant a church in order to graduate.[13] Denominations, missions, and churches may need to take some bold steps in revamping theological education institutions in order to produce the right type of leadership for church growth.

Model Of Leadership Training
For Growing Churches

As the Church seeks to extend itself in many different cultures and among thousands of people groups, it will need to carry out a flexible and dynamic pattern of leadership training. Churches will always grow much more rapidly when they are led by sensitive, aggressive, and responsible leaders. Thus, the training of pastors for church growth must be given high priority.[14]

David Hesselgrave observes that theological institutions cannot be counted on to give practical training for winning people to Christ, establishing them in local churches, and planting churches. He further observes that

> *The average curriculum contains a course in personal evangelism, a section of a course in systematic theology given over to ecclesiology, a few lessons of a course in practical theology devoted to evangelistic campaigns, and a general course in missions.*[15]

One positive development is that a number of Bible institutes and seminaries are now offering courses in church growth. While this may be the case, most curricula that are designed to train persons for the ministry in North America do not require a course on church growth. In most programs that train persons for the ministry a church growth course would be an elective. That fact alone indicates the need for the Church to be reformed in its orientation to ministry and the needs of the world. Since the "pastor of the local church is the key person for church growth, the training of the pastor becomes a crucial consideration."[16]

The issue of theological training in relationship to church growth is not necessarily the issue of the basic type of structure, whether it is the residential model, theological education by extension type, or the on-the-job model such as that used by the Pentecostals in Latin America. The effectiveness of a training program must be evaluated in terms of its success in serving the growth of the Church. The model of theological education that is chosen should be adopted because it contributes to rapid growth of the Church. This type of model, with church growth orientation, requires a thorough and creative pattern of leadership training. This will require a radical shift from a total emphasis on the traditional "content-oriented" curriculum to include a more "pragmatic-dynamic" method of training leaders, whether it is the training of full-time pastors, evangelists, teachers or local lay leaders. A church growth-oriented model must strive for a balance in the training program between content learning (academic knowledge) and basic ministry skills (know-how), which of course includes the practical knowledge of church growth.

Thus theological education, of whatever model, is not for maintaining the Church, or for filling pulpit vacancies. In fact Melvin Hodges suggests that there should be more workers trained than there are churches. As a result more workers will be available to plant new churches. If a person is trained with the idea that they will just fill a pulpit, it is very unlikely they will have personal initiative for church planting.[17] While academic credit will always be a part of theological education in many nations, the Church and its theological institutions need to give greater consideration to demanding competencies that their leaders will need in ministry.[18] It would not be unreasonable for the Church to require certain basic skills in church growth and church planting.

Academic credentials are not a requirement for Pentecostal leaders in Latin America. Proven leadership gifts and abilities are the necessary credentials. The burden of proof is in the fact that the Pentecostals are experiencing spectacular growth throughout Latin America. While they may be criticized for a lack of depth in their knowledge of Bible and theology, it is evident that they have excelled in the doing of ministry, namely, evangelism and church planting. The Pentecostals are not ignorant of academic opportunities for theological training. Yet they continue to shy away from this more formal means of education.

Three reasons can be given as to why the Pentecostals resist academic methods of learning. First, they continue to grow without any stress on theological academics. Their emphasis on practical application of the Bible has proved effective up to now. Secondly, the non-Pentecostals with all their academic training have not had the results to the degree that has been experienced by the Pentecostals. The third reason given by the Pentecostals is that many of their members have gone off to the theological institutions and have not returned with their same original drive and motivation.[19] It must be added that the Pentecostals are not necessarily against education itself. Rather, they are skeptical of the method of education that does not produce solid church growth.

The lesson is that theological education can actually hinder church growth. There has been the tendency of theological education, particularly the residential model, to produce graduates who are scholars and professionals rather than evangelists, preachers, teachers, and church planters.[20] Thus, every theological institution, of whatever type, should be judged both by the quality of the graduate and even more importantly by the quality of church growth that is experienced in the churches that the institution serves.

Finally, there is the issue of planning the leadership training needs for the future of the Church. The projections must grow out of plans for church growth. A denomination or association of churches must plan and coordinate its resources for leadership training on the basis of growth rate that is projected.[21]

---

[1]Wolff, *Man at the Top*, p. 116.

[2]Lois McKinney, "Leadership: Key to the Growth of the Church," in *Discipling through Theological Education by Extension*, ed. Vergil Gerber (Chicago: Moody Press, 1980), p. 179.

CHAPTER VI

The Administration Of Leadership In Church Growth

Leadership is the greatest need of the Church according to Richard G. Hutcheson, Jr. in his book, *Wheel Within the Wheel: Confronting the Management Crisis of the Pluralistic Church*. He observes that as a voluntary organization the Church expresses

> . . . *its belief in voluntarism theologically in terms of the faith response to grace and the priesthood of all believers. . . . Professionalism of the clergy . . . brings benefits, but also dangers.*[1]

It is therefore exceedingly important that leaders at every level of the Church see their function as that of serving all believers for the glory of God. This kind of spiritual leadership will administer and manage so that the Church will grow. The leadership of the Church administers in order that the Church functions according to its Biblical role and nature. Thus, a properly functioning leadership will lead to a properly functioning Church which will then result in quantitative and qualititative growth.

The leadership of the Church must administer for church growth in keeping with culturally relevant leadership styles. No one style of administration can be made normative for the church. Hendrik Kraemer points out the importance of this issue when he states that

> . . . the necessity of making a creative and critical, but free and courageous, use of existing and serviceable indigenous social forms and of methods of fostering spiritual life for the building of the Church, is at once self-evident and stringent.[2]

Role Of Organizational Leadership In Church Growth

The Church is a living spiritual organism. It has taken on many forms as it has manifested itself from place to place in various cultures. All organisms must have organization in order to function. And by necessity the Church also must have organization.

Although the Church has an organizational pattern, its organization is different from that of any other organization — at least it is supposed to be. The Church as an organization is different because it has a higher allegiance. The Church's organization not only serves those in the Church, but it also serves the world; and more importantly, it ultimately serves to glorify God.[3]

The responsibility of the Church's leadership is to see that organism and organization are kept in their proper balance. The Church must continually engage in teaching, preaching, worship, prayer, fellowship, giving, service, winning, and loving. The need for buildings, equipment, programs, committees and the like will vary from time to time.[4] The leadership of the Church has the responsibility to maintain the proper balance in the meeting of needs so the Church achieves the maximum inward and outward growth.

The Church's organization can and must give direction to its movement. Eugene Nida makes the appropriate observation that "many good movements have been killed by overorganization."[5] Too much organization can rob the Church of the energy necessary for a continued forward movement of growth. Hollis Green, in discussing why churches die, notes that:

> *Maintaining things as they are becomes the actual purpose of the Church. This over-institutionalization causes the Church to exist to preserve itself rather than to be creatively involved in winning the world.*[6]

The tendency for a drift toward a greater concern for preservation and maintenance, than for the missionary purpose for which the Church is designed, is sometimes referred to as "institutional drift."

A congregation can inadvertently move away from mission goals to maintenance goals when it makes the move into its own permanent building. Because the building is such a visible and commanding goal when it is completed, the completion leaves the congregation both satisfied and without a clear sense of continuing goals. So without realizing it, the shift from mission goals to a maintenance orientation begins. The result is that outreach tapers off and the growth of the congregation levels off.

Another area where the shift toward maintenance can occur relates to the leadership staff of a congregation. This can happen in adding a second person to the pastoral staff to serve as a minister of Christian education. Floyd Bartel in his book, *A New Look at Church Growth*, notes that church growth researchers have uncovered this tendency towards maintenance in enough formerly growing churches that they investigated the reasons. They discovered that this shift occured when a congregation added another pastoral staff member for nurture ministries. The result is that this organizational approach tips the balance away from evangelism to nurture, and growth stops. Thus, to administrate for growth, the second pastoral staff person should be a minister of outreach/church growth and the third staff person a minister of Christian education.[7] If the minister of outreach/church growth knows his church growth principles and serves as an effective enabler in helping the laity use their gifts for ministry, the congregation will be blessed of God and will grow.

It is extremely easy for leadership to turn their attention inward and become preoccupied with maintenance of the Church's organization. In order to avoid this tendency Win Arn in his book, *The Pastor's Church Growth Handbook*, has suggested the following four steps:

> *1. Develop a clear statement of purpose — a philosophy of ministry — for your church; one that directly relates the church and its reason for existence to God's unswerving purpose — the redemption of lost mankind.*
> *2. Translate this purpose into measurable goals . . . goals which become the basis for priorities, programming and organization in the church.*
> *3. Evaluate progress on a regular basis, as it relates to achieving these goals.*
> *4. Celebrate accomplishment. Enjoy success and achievement in reaching these goals. People are inspired and grow personally when they see tangible evidence of God's blessing in their church.*[8]

One of the important functions of the Church's organization is to plan for the future. The leadership must project future growth, plan accordingly, and then work to achieve it. Planning for church growth takes into consideration the need for such things as additional church staff, larger building facilities, and bigger parking lots.

Leadership cannot do all the work and expect the congregation to be alive and growing. Such an approach will stifle growth and extinguish life. David Womack points out that "Leaders must draw on the potential vitality of the whole body, and motivate all cells, organs, and systems to function in a healthy and coordinate manner."[9] Growth will result when leaders delegate authority and motivate great numbers of dedicated Christians.

The congregation's leadership must constantly seek the involvement of new and creative talent. In fact there is a direct relationship between the growth of a congregation and the amount of leadership that is available. Womack contends that " a premeditated development in the level of administration will often produce subsequent numerical increase."[10] And, according to Womack, many churches have failed to grow because they have not understood the simple rule "that organizational expansion always preceded numerical increase.[11] In other words, a congregation cannot grow beyond the administrative abilities of the pastor, staff, and lay leaders. A pastor with his staff and lay leaders can efficiently care for only a given number of people. Thus, when that level is reached, the Church will cease to grow.[12] It is not only excessive organization that can retard church growth, lack of organization can have the same effect.

Administering for church growth also involves the right number of pastoral staff and secretarial help. Charles Mylander in his book, *Secrets for Growing Churches*, speaks to this point by looking to the research by the religious sociologist, Richard A. Myers. This research has documented a crucial growth ratio between full-time equippers and actual attendance. This research developed the rule of thumb, $(1 + 1):200$, which means one pastor and one secretary for each 200 people in Sunday school attendance. When a congregation reaches that ratio, growth will often level off unless the congregation takes on another staff member. Myers also found that church growth was affected by the relationship between the number of paid staff members and the number of Sunday school classes. The research showed that a growing congregation will need a minimum of ten Sunday school classes for every full-time pastor. A congregation can then expect up to 200 people in Sunday school for every pastor.[13] There are always exceptions to the rule but it does offer practical help so that churches can plan for growth through the proper ratio of administrative staff to the growth goals of the congregation. It is not just a matter of how many people the full-time administrative staff can serve. The level of unpaid volunteer workers in the congregation will reach a certain number in relationship to the administrative staff. Mylander points out that:

> *In most churches the number of unpaid volunteers will not keep increasing without adding paid staff. And only as the number of lay leaders expands can the church keep growing.* [14]

The organizational administrative staff of a congregation is so important that understaffing will tend to weaken the life and program of the church and will lead to stagnated growth. Lyle Schaller notes that:

> *. . . in general there are four important responsibilities that often are neglected in large understaffed churches. One of these, the failure to assimilate new members into the fellowship of the church, is very common in large churches. A second is the lack of a consistent leadership development program to provide a continuing supply of competent and self-confident lay volunteers to replace the persons who move away or retire and to staff new ministries. A third deficit frequently produced by understaffing is in program. Many large congregations have too few classes, choirs, study groups, prayer cells, circles in the women's organization, youth fellowship, outreach programs and mission groups for the number of members. One result of underprogramming is an excessively large proportion of relatively inactive members. A fourth result of understaffing in many large churches is deterioration of the new member recruitment system because of staff neglect. When this phase of congregational life is understaffed, it is the equivalent of a decision to staff for a decline in the size of that congregation.* [15]

The organization must not be seen as an impediment to the smooth functioning of the Church. It is intended to be the very mechanism through which the shepherding of the Church and the outreach of the Church can be carried on. Thus, Jay Adams concludes that "Mismanagement, not organization, actually is the evil that so often constitutes the underlying difficulty."[16]

Role Of Denominational And Mission Leaders
In Church Growth

Leaders of The Christian and Missionary Alliance National Churches worldwide converged on Lima, Peru in March 1983 for The Alliance World Fellowship's quadrennial conference. It is a consultative group that meets to benefit from other churches' experiences and to consider current ecclesiastical interests. One noteworthy aspect of this event is that the Alliance constituency was encouraged to "Pray for these important meetings. They can mean much to church growth around the world."[17] Church growth is likely to occur if and when denominational and mission leaders see that one of the key functions is in that area.

The February 1981 issue of *Net Results*, a newsletter published by the National Evangelistic Association of the Christian Church (Disciples of Christ), carried a lead article entitled, "Denominational Executives Can Stimulate Growth." The denomination had experienced a quarter century of alarming decline in the thirty county Northeast area of Texas. In 1974 this declining trend was turned around and the seventy churches have increased from 8,290 in 1975 to 9,133 members in 1980. This great reversal came about when concerned leaders of these churches met in 1975 and decided to make congregational renewal and church growth the top priority.

The denominational leaders took two basic approaches to reverse the declining growth of the churches. The first approach was for the leaders to give special attention to salvaging as many of the very small congregations as possible. These struggling churches were encouraged to see their important role in the denomination. Various activities were organized between churches to encourage a wide fellowship. Upgraded pastoral care was provided to lead these small churches. The second approach to remedying this situation was to focus on church growth in all congregations, large and small. Among other things the following was carried out, as reported by the article:

> Growth-consciousness was fostered by publishing frequent lists of total additions by baptism and transfer in all area churches. Charts showing the growth curves of all area congregations were devised and displayed. Financial incentives were given for lay persons and ministers to attend evangelism workshops. These methods gradually created a positive "peer pressure" among the congregations to "get everyone in on the act."[18]

The most effective tool used by the denomination was to hold church growth seminars. The seminars were held not just for pastors or evangelism chairpersons but for the total membership insofar as possible. The seminars were generally scheduled as the program for an all-church dinner. In addition to the seminar the article recounts that:

> A booklet of mimeographed material tailored to each local church situation includes a graph of the congregation's past twenty-year growth pattern. Each participant receives a copy of the booklet for further study at home. Extra copies are provided so that the minister can use them in later review, additional training, or with persons absent from the seminar.[19]

After experiencing six years of exciting growth the denomination's leaders have again reaffirmed the priority of church growth. Another set of church growth seminars are planned to follow up those congregations which conducted the first seminar.[20]

Francis Dubose in his book, *How Churches Grow in an Urban World*, states that:

> *In the Baptist association, the chief administrative leader, usually known as the director of missions, should be a church growth specialist, or if not, should have such a specialist on his staff.*[21]

Carl Dudley in his book, *Where Have All Our People Gone?*, states that "Denominational decisions have a direct impact on the growth and decline of individual congregations."[22] Dudley seeks to support his statement by pointing out that certain attitudes and policies of the mainline churches have worked for or against growth.[23] The importance of denominational and mission leaders for the cause of church growth is also confirmed by the missiologist, David Hesselgrave. In regard to planting churches Hesselgrave suggests that organization for such an effort will provide direction in extending the frontiers of the Church. Within the organization leaders should be required to "take responsibility for planning strategy, and gathering and deploying human and financial resources for the task,"[24] Organizational leadership is so important that Hesselgrave gives this very apt word:

> *Home-mission leaders must resist the temptation to become only, or primarily, caretakers of the churches already established. Some of their most important functions should be to encourage an overall plan for church extension, to suggest ways and means of carrying out the plan, and to provide leadership in implementation.*[25]

The best articulation of this issue has been made by Ernest Miller, the editor of *Net Results* newsletter that is published by the National Evangelism Association of the Christian Church (Disciples of Christ). He points out that if his denomination is going to grow, all expressions of the denomination must facilitate growth. He continues by saying:

Congregations, except isolated ones under special circumstances, will not grow without the leadership from national and regional levels of the denomination. Such leadership must come from changes in structure and in the functions of leadership that produce a posture for growth. A structure is needed, the very function of which produces growth — rather than structure that adds growth as something annexed or adds extra programs for evangelism and special drives for new congregations. Each regional and national expression of the church can build a structure, arrange its staff, and order financing so that its very functioning will produce growth.

Just as there are identifiable strategies which, when implemented by local churches, produce growth; there are identifiable strategies which, when implemented by the entire denomination, will produce growth.[26]

Miller suggests a list of traits or structural patterns which produce growth in a denomination or fellowship of churches. The following list, suggested by Miller, could also be taken as a set of basic or long-range goals:

1. A large number of denominational executives will believe that God wants their part of Christ's Church to serve his purposes in today's world with growing, expanding congregations rather than as a faithful remnant that maintains its numbers.

*2. Denominational executives will clearly distinguish between growth posture and maintenance posture and implement changes that put the church in a posture **known** to produce growth.*

3. Growth will be set as a high priority. Denominational executives will place at the top of national and regional agendas those growth traits which can be brought into being by their present leadership authority and influence.

4. The election and employment of national and regional leaders will be based on "matters of competence, accountability, and responsiveness to and awareness of the work of the local churches."

5. Denominational executives will be efficient in train-
ing "pastors to serve and resource their laity" for growth.
6. The denomination will have a posture that develops
and finances new congregations, not through funds es-
pecially raised for that purpose at a given time, but as
the common and constant outgrowth of their normal
procedures.
7. The seminaries who train young ministers will be
knowledgeable in "staffing local churches for growth."
They will help students distinguish between staffing for
maintenance and staffing for growth, with a constant em-
phasis on staffing for growth.
8. All regional and national expressions of the Church
will encourage continual dialogue, training, and im-
plementation of those ingredients in local church pro-
grams which produce growth in their setting.[27]

Miller summarizes his concern for denominational leadership in church growth by stating that local churches will find growth difficult or impossible if they get no help from that leadership.[28] This means that independent churches face the liability of having to go it on their own.

In light of this challenge for church leaders there are encouraging signs, according to Peter Wagner, with the emergence of a cadre of professional church diagnosticians whom he calls "ecclesiologists."[29] According to Wagner these professionals have a combination of aptitude, training, and intuition to be able to examine a congregation and diagnose its health in approximately one day's time, given some previous research and measurements by the pastor. These experts are found in some denominations and some work independently to assist interdenominational churches.[30] This means that any congregation, whether denominational or independent, can get help to chart a new course for growth.

Role Of Pastor In Church Growth

Jesus Christ said that He would build His Church and the gates of hell would not prevail against it. This means that every pastor is important enough in Christ's program "to be under obligation to give his very best and **most** to **make things happen** in his local church."[31] The eminent missiologist, George Peters, says that leadership "may well be the main key to church growth and health."[32] Another missiologist, Peter Wagner, speaks of vital signs of healthy churches. Churches, like human beings, have certain "vital signs that seem to be common among those that are healthy and growing."[33] The first out of seven vital signs of a healthy congregation, according to Wagner, is that of the pastoral leadership. A congregation can score well on four or five of the seven vital signs and perhaps grow. But Wagner says that there are four axioms of church growth and if a congregation is not meeting even one of the axoims, they cannot expect to grow well. The first of four axoims is that "the pastor must want the church to grow and be willing to pay the price. . . . The pastor is the person who is key to the growth of the local church."[34] C. B. Hogue in, *I Want My Church to Grow*, supports the idea that the pastor is the key when he says:

> *The most influential voice in the life of the church comes from the pulpit. Several times each week, the pastor has an opportunity to share his vision of the church and its mission. If he speaks with God-given assurance and urgency, the pastor can, through his weekly sermons, motivate, encourage, challenge, inspire, and infect his people with his insights into the good news. As the acknowledged leader of most churches, the pastor can profoundly shape the ministry of his congregation. In normal situations, the church assumes the pastor's attributes and attitudes.*[35]

After extensive research there has been only one lone voice that downplays the role of the pastor. Lyle Schaller makes the statement that "the church growth movement overstates the importance of the minister in terms of church growth. I don't think the minister is quite that influential."[36] He does not, however, explain the reason for his opinion.

Church growth surveys are overwhelming in their evidence that the pastor is one of the main keys to growth. C. B. Hogue refers to a survey taken of fifteen fast-growing churches. The key factor in numerical increase in eleven of the churches was the pastor. In nine of the churches new pastoral leadership meant a sudden spurt in growth.[37] Wendell Belew in his book, *Churches and How They Grow*, gives descriptions of innovative congregational programs. After examining the growth of a number of churches Belew concludes by saying:

> *In all these instances of growth (although the pastor has been unwilling to note his own importance), the growth has taken place because of the pastor's concept of God, the church, his calling, and his ability through the power of the Holy Spirit to motivate his church.*[38]

Allen Swanson did ten case studies of church growth in Taiwan and found that in most of the churches studied, effective programs for church growth were found to be the direct results of the vision and burden of one man — the pastor. In relation to the pastor's role in church growth Swanson says that:

> *It would be difficult to overstate the importance of this one man in each of the growing churches. Not that he was a one-man show. Indeed, quite the opposite. Being strong he was yet aware of potential leadership around him and set his hand to the development of strong men to share the task. However, the vision commitment and sense of confidence inspired by God's chosen leader has been the key factor to successful growth in nearly every church studied.*[39]

In the Church today the pastor is generally recognized as the primary leader. "He is responsible to God, the congregation, and himself. He cannot do all the work, but he must see that all the work is done.[40] John English in his book, *The Minister and His Ministry*, says that

95

> *. . . a church is as good as its minister. The teaching of the New Testament is clear and emphatic that the pastor of a church is its official, leader, and in what that leadership consists.*[41]

Christ leads His Church through these undershepherds. Both the leaders of the Church and those whom they lead take orders directly from Christ who is the Chief Shepherd. The Chief Shepherd calls and ordains these leaders. He has delegated to them His authority to lead and manage the Church. "This authority is great, yet limited; and it is entirely delegated."[42]

According to Arthur Adams in *Pastoral Administration*, the pastor's responsibility is plainly an administrative task.[43] James Currin, in writing on leadership, takes a slightly different view saying that "the historical development of the Church has brought with it administrative functions for the pastor."[44] Thomas Campbell in his book, *The Gift of Administration*, speaks to this issue in his concern that the role of the clergy not undermine the centrality of the doctrine of the priesthood of all believers and thus weaken the effectiveness of the Church. Campbell suggests that the clergy be defined around the gift of administration, and doing so will clarify the clergy role, support and enrich the priesthood of all believers.[45] Peter Wagner distinguishes between the gift of administrations in 1 Corinthians 12:28 and the gift of leadership in Romans 12:8. Wagner feels "that a church-growth pastor can get along without the gift of administration but not without the gift of leadership."[46] He contends that growth potential is limited unless the person called to head up the congregation has the gift of leadership.[47] The terms "administration" and "leadership" are different in meaning but may very well overlap in function. To administrate may very well involve at least some leadership and to lead may very well involve at least some administration. The degree to which a pastor leads and administrates will involve his or her personality and the combination of spiritual gifts that he or she possesses. The pastor, as leader, certainly must administrate. He or she should be supported by lay leaders who can pick up the slack in the areas of leadership and administration where the pastor needs support. A growing congregation is one where both the leadership and administration of the pastor are supported by lay leaders. Thus, a congregation that has full-orbed leadership and administration will most certainly grow.

There is another more basic area where there may need to be a more important distinction than between the matter of leadership and administration. Peter Wagner has suggested that in the pastor's ministry there are two basic areas of service, leadership roles and ministry roles. He has related both role areas to church growth. In the split-image spectrum that portrays the leadership role (Figure 2), moving to the left the pastor is the primary leader, and toward the right the

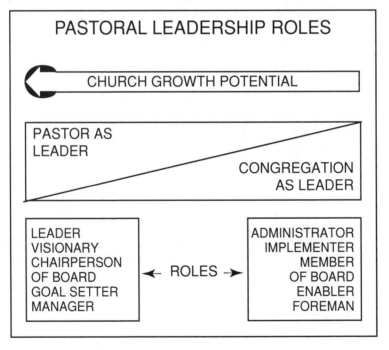

Figure 2[48]

congregation controls the leadership. The cultural, socio-economic, denominational, and personality factors will determine how far the pastor will move to the left or right. Wagner, rightly so, contends that a pastor toward the left end of the range will have a better growth potential in his ministry, other things being equal. To each side of the leadership spectrum Wagner has given several pairs of labels to identify the type of leader a pastor will be at either side of the spectrum.[49] The important thing for church growth is that the pastor try to be the kind of leader he or she should be in order to see the maximum amount of growth. Wagner's explanation of the labels, as they relate to church growth are as follows:

> The church has a higher potential for growth if the pastor is a leader more than he is an administrator. A leader, as the next pair of labels indicates, is a visionary; while an administrator is an implementor of someone else's vision.
>
> A church growth pastor is a goal-setter; less growth potential is predicted for a pastor with the self-image of an "enabler," who encourages the lay people to set the goals.
>
> To use an industrial model, the pastor who tends to be more a manager type than a foreman type will enhance the growth possibilities for the church.[50]

The other area of the pastor's work is that of a ministry role as illustrated by a second split-image spectrum (Figure 3). This area of ministry involves the pastor in matching people to service that corresponds with their God-given ministry role. To the left side of the spectrum the pastor carries out most of the ministry within the congregation. But, as Wagner notes, the growth potential increases as the pastor becomes less involved in carrying the burden of ministry in the congregation and more committed to leading the membership in active service. This then involves every believer using their spiritual gifts for the life of the body. The pastor, of course, uses his or her gifts, but a pastor who is concerned for growth will give attention to

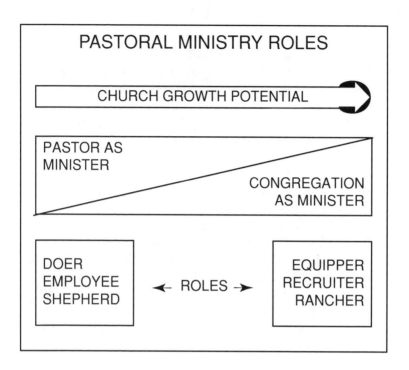

Figure 3[51]

each believer actively using their gift.[52] "The pastor is more of an equipper for ministry than a doer of ministry."[53] The pastor is not the employee of the congregation but instead a coordinator of the believers as they carry out the work of the ministry. It is summed up by Peter Wagner:

> *Thus, the pastor's major role for growth is to lead. The congregation's major role for growth is to do the ministry. Although maintaining the proper relationship between the two will not solve every growth problem for every church, it will help unlock tremendous opportunities for growth.*[54]

Another factor that affects the role of the pastor in church growth is the length of pastorate. Three is no evidence that long pastorates necessarily result in church growth. On the other hand a congregation will not experience sustained growth without the benefit of an adequately lengthy pastorate.[55] Extensive research on a number of growing churches throughout North America showed that churches with strong growth had pastorates of from five to twelve years. If this be the case it means that many churches, particularly the many smaller congregations, fail to realize their potential in growth because their pastors serve for such short periods.[56] When a congregation is growing, one of the biggest threats to that growth is a change of pastors. "Short pastorates tend to encourage peaks and valleys in the congregation's growth pattern."[57] One of the common characteristics of small churches is that they have a frequency of pastoral changes. The short pastorate, of less than five years, is a serious threat to the development of a sustained growth rate. One authority has stated that the fifth, sixth, seventh, and eighth years are generally the most productive years of a pastor's ministry. Obviously because of the divine element in ministry the length of a fruitful pastorate may vary from the five to eight year time frame. But it is clear that many congregations have failed to reach their full potential in growth because of pastorates that are too brief.[58]

Every local congregation has the right to demand that their pastor be informed of, and work for, church growth. To highlight the importance of the pastor's role in that realm, Hogue has suggested what he calls, "Pastor's Personal Commitment" (Figure 4), that a pastor would make to his congregation as a covenent.

> *"I have studied carefully the biblical responsibilities given to me from the New Testament. I have developed a vision for growing a great church. I believe that God wants the church to grow both numerically and in a loving Christlike evangelistic ministry. Believing this, I make the following spiritual, intellectual, emotional, and physical commitment of myself to God and to growing a great evangelistic church:*

(1) I commit myself to be a witness as my lifestyle and to develop my own personal spiritual life through prayer, Bible study, and meditation.

(2) I commit myself to continuing Bible study and prayer for feeding the flock of God.

(3) I commit myself to a growing understanding of the theology-vision of growing an evangelistic church.

(4) I commit myself to sharing the vision with individuals and groups within the church until the body of the church is permeated with a philosophy of evangelistic growth.

(5) I commit myself to enlist and involve an evangelism leadership group to implement growing an evangelistic church.

(6) I commit myself to the administrative oversight of equipping the saints to do the work of ministry as the pastor-equipper of the church.''

_____

(Signed)

_____

(Date)

Figure 4 Pastor's Personal Commitment[59]

The importance of the pastor's role in the growth of the congregation he serves cannot be overestimated. The importance of the pastor has been summed up well by Elmer Town when he says:

> *A church is always built **by** a man, but is never built **on** a man. Churches started by committees never seem to prosper. God's grace and power must be poured into a man — God's servant. Remember, "A great church is always **caused**, it never just happens." God always has his servant who sacrifices, prays and works.*[60]

101

Role Of Lay Leaders In Church Growth

One of the key factors in the growth of the early Church was the involvement of lay leadership. The Church entered Antioch on the feet of laymen from Cyprus and Cyrene. The Church in Rome got its start through the efforts of lay leaders. Roger Hedlund, in analyzing why churches grow in India, notes that in Andra state the movement of caste Hindus to Christ was largely spontaneous and led by lay persons — lay leadership being a key factor in the spread of the gospel.[61] Whether in the first century or in the twentieth century, indigenous leadership is very important. Congregations experience more stable growth when the leadership is part of the local community. Thus, for the sake of healthy growth the transition to indigenous leadership should be made as rapidly as possible in every church planting situation.[62]

Most pastors feel the urgent need in their congregation for lay leaders who are competent, committed, and dependable. The greatest sense of frustration for some pastors is the discovering, recruiting, and training of lay leaders who will take substantive roles in the congregation. The pastor's leadership ability is put to test as he or she seeks to inspire and train consecrated and gifted lay leadership.[63] A lesson from the New Testament shows that Paul did not expect lay leaders to be fully qualified on their own. For that reason he taught and trained them. Paul appointed elders in the churches that he planted (Acts 14:21-25). Paul also began to recruit especially gifted men to teach and train, such as Mark and Timothy. So Paul not only trained leaders "in the churches," but also trained leaders "for the churches."[64] So it is not just the need for lay leadership that is important but even more crucial is the need for trained leadership. "Teaching the correct things in the beginning days of the church will result in the right kind of leadership and proper growth."[65]

Churches will not grow unless there is a corps of volunteer lay leaders whose major ministry is directed toward the unsaved.[66] In fact, John Uhlig has clearly stated the issue when he says that churches experience rapid growth

. . . because they have dedicated laity excited with the potential of their church and very aware that if their congregation is going to minister to its community, they are the ones responsible to God for its effective leadership.[67]

Each congregation needs a strong corps of level two leaders, in keeping with McGavran's definition of levels of leaders.[68] It is impossible to calculate the potential for growth in the Church of Jesus Christ if there were a mobilization of level two workers. The level two lay worker is the unpaid volunteer who heads out and away from the congregation for his or her primary ministry. These lay leaders are able to relate with persons outside the local church family. Thus, they enjoy being involved with outreach activities that are not maintenance-oriented. They know unreached people in the community and purposefully maintain contact with them.

A growing congregation mobilizes and encourages these leaders. A sensitive pastor along with his lay leaders will avoid giving maintenance responsibilities to the leaders who are gifted for outreach.[69] Generally there is no problem of leadership involvement in ministering to the congregation for inward qualitative growth. It seems to be a human tendency for the leadership to be more concerned with inward qualitative growth rather than reaching out. An imbalance in leadership levels will generally lead to arrested growth. Most congregations will tend to have an overabundance of level one leaders (those who carry on the maintenance ministry of the congregation) and too few level two leaders.[70]

Recruiting, equipping, and deploying of level two leaders will take sensitivity and effort. The pastor and other lay leaders must recruit such leaders in the congregation whose gifts are such that they know how to relate to the unsaved. Rather than being intimidated, they are motivated to get out into the world for outreach ministries. Some of the best level two leaders come from those who have recently come to Christ and into the Church. Most of their friends are unsaved. They know the best methods of communication to use in reaching and relating to the unsaved. Other level two leaders can be recruited from level one leaders. Some of these level one leaders have the capacity to function both in and outside the church walls. Some level one leaders, who are mature and especially gifted, could be encouraged to take on a level two leadership role.[71] Charles Chaney and Ron Lewis in their book, *Design for Church Growth*, suggest the following ways in which level two[72] leaders can be equipped and deployed:

> *Avoid overinvolvement of the Class II worker in Class I work.*
> *Train the Class II worker to keep in touch with unchurched people.*
> *Develop the natural skills of the Class II worker for reaching the unchurched.*
> *Have special Bible studies for Class II workers. Use curriculum materials that are outreach oriented.*
> *Plan social activities designed along guidelines given by Class II workers.*
> *Constantly interview Class II workers to find material and strategies that create a response among the unchurched.*
> *Give regular support and affirmation to the Class II leader.*
> *Accept irregular attendance at church activities by Class II workers.*
> *Provide the program and atmosphere in the church that will minister to those reached through the ministry of the Class II worker.*[73]

Relating to the recruiting and equipping these leaders Mahlon Hillard has a very apt word:

> *The first item to consider might be helping the layman realize he has a gift and ministry to be developed and used before God. To train in **this** manner is not once-a-year message presentation. Rather, this teaching must be a major part of a pastor's emphasis. Many know this basic Bible principle, but it must be stressed continually for*

results. Many have been tutored that only a few really minister, and it takes time to overcome this thinking. People's thought patterns can change — and the most thrilling change is to see a layman realize **he** *is a minister and has a gift to be used of God.*[74]

[1]Richard G. Hutcheson, Jr. *Wheel Within the Wheel: Confronting the Management Crisis of the Pluralistic Church* (Atlanta: John Knox Press, 1979), p. 182.

[2]Hendrick Kraemer, *The Christian Message in a Non-Christian World* (Grand Rapids: Kregel Publications, 1938), p. 421.

[3]Theodore Wilhelm Engstrom and Edward R. Dayton, *The Art of Management for Christian Leaders* (Waco: Word Books, Publisher, 1976), pp. 15-16.

[4]Gaines S. Dobbins, *Building Better Churches* (Nashville: Broadman Press, 1947), p. 141.

[5]Eugene A. Nida, *Message and Mission* (New York: Harper & Row Publishers, 1960), p. 151.

[6]Green, *Why Churches Die: A Guide to Basic Evangelism and Church Growth*, p. 65.

[7]Floyd G. Bartel, *A New Look at Church Growth* (Newton, Kan.: Faith and Life Press, 1979), pp. 22-23.

[8]Win Arn, *The Pastor's Church Growth Handbook* (Pasadena: Institute for American Church Growth, 1979), p. 198.

[9]David A. Womack, *The Pyramid Principle of Church Growth* (Minneapolis: Bethany Fellowship, Inc., 1977), p. 22.

[10]Ibid., p. 79.

[11]Ibid., p. 80.

[12]Ibid., pp. 80-81.

[13]Charles Mylander, *Secrets for Growing Churches* (San Francisco: Harper & Row, Publishers, 1979), pp. 58-59.

[14]Ibid., p. 105.

[15]Lyle E. Schaller, *The Multiple Staff and the Larger Church* (Nashville: Abingdon, 1980), pp. 58-59.

[16]Adams, *Pastoral Leadership*, p. 12.

[17]"Lima Hosts Alliance World Fellowship," *Alliance World Prayer Line*, March 1983, p. 1.

[18]"Denominational Executives Can Stimulate Growth," *Net Results*, February 1981, Vol. 1, No. 7, p. 1.

[19]Ibid., p. 4.

[20]Ibid.

[21]Francis M. Dubose, *How Churches Grow in an Urban World* (Nashville: Broadman Press, 1978), p. 156.

[22]Carl S. Dudley, *Where Have All Our People Gone?* (New York: The Pilgrim Press, 1979), p. 81.

[23]Ibid., pp. 81-82.

[24]Hesselgrave, *Planting Churches Cross-Culturally: A Guide for Home and Foreign Missions*, p. 86.

[25]Ibid., pp. 85-86.

[26]Ernest Miller, "Church Growth Compared to Caterpillar," *Net Results*, December 1980, p. 3.

[27]Ibid.

[28]Ibid.

[29]C. Peter Wagner, *Your Church Can Be Healthy* (Nashville: Abingdon, 1979), p. 20.

[30]Ibid.

[31]Riggs, *Make it Happen*, p. 13.

[32]George W. Peters, *A Theology of Church Growth* (Grand Rapids: Zondervan Publishing House, 1981), p. 238.

[33]Wagner, *Your Church Can Be Healthy*, p. 21.

[34]Ibid., pp. 21, 24.

[35]C. B. Hogue, *I Want My Church to Grow* (Nashville: Broadman, 1977), p. 66.

[36]Lyle Schaller, "The Changing Focus of Church Finances," *Leadership* 2 (Spring 1981):24.

[37]Hogue, *I Want My Church to Grow*, p. 66.

[38]M. Wendell Belew, *Churches and How They Grow* (Nashville: Broadman Press, 1981), p. 41.

[39]Allen Swanson, ed., *I Will Build My Church: Ten Case Studies of Church Growth in Taiwan* (Pasadena: William Carey Library, 1977), p. 170.

[40]James H. Currin, "The Leadership of Churches," in *The Birth of Churches*, ed. Talmadge R. Amberson (Nashville: Broadman, 1979), p. 131.

[41]English, *The Minister and His Ministry*, p. 29.

[42]Adams, *Pastoral Leadership*, p. 13.

[43]Adams, *Pastoral Administration*, pp. 13-14.

[44]Currin, "The Leadership of Churches," pp. 131-32.

[45]Thomas G. Campbell, *The Gift of Administration* (Philadelphia: The Westminster Press, 1981), p. 17.

[46]Wagner, *Your Spiritual Gifts Can Help Your Church Grow*, p. 156.

[47]Ibid.

[48]Wagner, "*Good Pastors Don't Make Churches Grow*," p. 68.

[49]Ibid.

[50]Ibid., p. 69.

[51]Ibid., p. 71.

[52]Ibid., pp. 71-72.

[53]Ibid., p. 72.

[54]Ibid.

[56]Lyle E. Schaller, *Assimilating New Members* (Nashville: Abingdon, 1978), p. 127.

[56]Orjala, *Get Ready to Grow: A Strategy for Local Church Growth*, p. 97.

[57]Schaller, *Assimilating New Members*, p. 127.

[58]Orjala, *Get Ready to Grow: A Strategy for Local Church Growth*, p. 97.

[59]Hogue, *I Want My Church to Grow*, p. 157.

[60]Towns, *Getting A Church Started in the Face of Insurmountable Odds with Limited Resources in Unlikely Circumstances*, p. 12.

[61]Roger E. Hedlund, "Why Do Churches in India Grow?" *Asia Theological News*, July-September 1982, p. 19.

[62]Lockwood, "The Growth of Churches," p. 156.

[63]Dobbins, *Building Better Churches*, p. 243.

[64]Lockwood, "The Growth of Churches," p. 157.

[65]Ibid.

[66]Chaney and Lewis, *Design for Church Growth*, p. 107.

[67]John Uhlig, "Growth-Restricting Obstacles: How to Find and Overcome Them," in *The Pastor's Church Growth Handbook*, ed. Win Arn (Pasadena: Church Growth Press, 1979), p. 69.

[68]See Chapter five for the types of leaders as defined by Donald McGavran and Lois McKinney.

107

[69]Chaney and Lewis, *Design for Church Growth*, pp. 51, 133.

[70]Ibid., p. 51.

[71]Ibid., p. 133.

[72]The terms "level" and "class" are used interchangeably.

[73]Chaney and Lewis, *Design for Church Growth*, pp. 133-34.

[74]Mahlon Hillard, "Mark Twain and the Leadership Church," *The Standard*, May 1, 1973, p. 27.

CHAPTER VII

The Task Of Leadership In Church Growth

The task of leadership in church growth can be effectively carried out if the leader is the right kind of person doing the right thing. It is a balance of being and doing. The effective leader must first of all be the right kind of person in order to qualify as one whom God can use. Thus, the leader must possess certain spiritual qualities and leadership abilities so that his or her ministry will be effective for the cause of church growth. For this reason the characteristics of church growth leadership will be examined prior to the discussion of the actual functions that must be carried out.

Characteristics Of Church Growth Leadership

Spiritual Qualities

Church growth leaders are not really the "superstar" type of pastor. God does not promise the Church this type of person. He does, however, promise to provide all necessary leaders who are equipped with gifts of the Spirit. If churches feel that they must depend on pastoral "superstars" for growth, there is a fundamental misunderstanding about the Church of Jesus Christ.[1]

Certain spiritual qualities are a basic characteristic of church growth leadership. First, church growth leaders must have a biblical understanding about salvation. They must be convinced that people are lost without Christ, that God desires all to be saved, and that the way of salvation is through repentance and faith in Christ.[2]

Second, church growth leaders must be committed to evangelism. They take the Lordship of Jesus Christ seriously so that they are willing to pay the price for doing whatever is necessary to obey and fulfill Christ's Great Commission.

Third, church growth leaders must be persons of faith. Church growth leaders might be intimidated by the charge that they are "triumphalists," but they are convinced that Christ is building His Church.[3] Without faith that God wants evangelism carried out, and without the faith that He will help us do it, little happens. The kind of faith needed for growth leadership goes far beyond self-confidence, positive thinking, or optimism. It is a faith that is centered in God who can work in spite of our weaknesses.[4] Church growth results are achieved because leaders see with "church growth eyes" the possibilities God has for their congregation and then by faith determine to meet specific goals of growth. A vision for growth usually involves "leaps of faith."

Fourth, church growth leaders must pray for growth. They are burdened for particular people who become a target of prayer in a consistent pattern. They pray for God's guidance and wisdom for the design of evangelistic strategy and methodologies.

Fifth, church growth leaders must recognize their important function in a humble spirit. Peter Wagner makes note of the fact that "It is normal for the pastor of a growing church to deny that he is a primary key to growth."[5] They know that growth is not solely because of their efforts. They recognize the essential contribution of every other person who is involved in the congregation's growth. A humble church growth pastor will be careful to make sure that the people of the congregation are well aware of his or her dependence on them.

J. Oswald Sanders in his book, *Spiritual Leadership*, points out that natural leadership and spiritual leadership have many points of similarity but in certain aspects they may be antithetical. A church growth leader must strive to avoid those natural characteristics and seek the spiritual ones. Sanders shows the differences in the natural and spiritual:

Natural	Spiritual
Self-confident	Confident in God
Knows men	Also knows God
Makes own decisions	Seeks to find God's will
Ambitious	Self-effacing
Originates own methods	Finds and follows God's methods
Enjoys commanding others	Delights to obey God
Motivated by personal considerations	Motivated by love for God and man
Independent	God-dependent[6]

Leadership Abilities

There is a running debate among leadership theorists whether leaders are born or made. Sanders seems to have advanced the most balanced answer when he says:

> *It would appear that the correct answer is, "Both."*
> *Leadership has been defined as an "elusive and electric quality" that comes directly from God. On the other hand, it is clear that leadership skills can be cultivated and developed. Each of us from birth possesses skills that either qualify or disqualify us for certain tasks. Those skills often lie dormant until some crisis calls forth their exercise. They can and should be developed.*[7]

111

It is not the lack of skill that holds leaders back from growth leadership. Conviction comes first and skill comes second.[8] Although leadership competence is not unimportant, skills do not make the impact that a leader's attitude does. Enthusiasm has positive effects on the leaders and their congregations. Attitude can be contagious. Effective church growth leadership will project an image of enthusiasm for growth of the Church.[9] A church growth leader is a possibility thinker whose dynamic leadership catalyzes the entire denomination or congregation into action for growth.[10] Thus, effective church growth leadership generates enthusiasm in the congregation for church growth.

Church growth leadership has a vision for growth and communicates it to the people of God. It is a vision that sees the possibilities and consequently leads to applying appropriate strategies to gain maximum results in the expansion of the Church. With such vision the leaders and the people in the pew are not satisfied with doing the "busy work" of the Church.[11] When the Church becomes increasingly institutional and develops more and more interest in its own maintenance, the desire of the leaders seems to shift toward more organizational concerns rather than retaining a vision for church growth. However, a leader who would give leadership to the mission of the Church must have a vision for growth. They must see God's missionary mandate to the Church as central to its reason for existence in this world and in turn communicate this to his/her followers.[12]

In addition to a vision for growth, growing churches have purposeful, goal-directed, achievement-oriented leadership. Such leaders "are not reluctant to set measurable goals and to allow their success or failure to be evaluated in the light of these goals."[13] In addition they have the ability to motivate and organize people to work together in striving for the goals.

Church growth leaders use various approaches in their leadership styles but the end result of their style is growth. Any approach to leadership is acceptable so long as it produces genuine growth. The leadership approach will vary greatly according to the particular cultural context. Each leader's personality, gifts and culture affect his or her functioning. The bottom line is that the leadership is culturally relevant and produces growth in the Church.[14]

Functions Of Church Growth Leadership

The New Testament does not give a once-for-all leadership pattern for the function of the Church's leaders. The New Testament portrays a number of leadership patterns that were culturally appropriate. The leadership patterns ranged from a communal approach (Acts 2:42-47) to, apparently, leadership by a council of "apostles and elders" (Acts 15:4, 6, 22), to the more highly structured patterns in the pastoral epistles. In each case the leadership pattern developed in response to the felt needs of the members of the culture and subculture in which the particular congregation operated. Most crucial and basic to the growth of the Church is a leadership that functions in a culturally relevant way. Thus the Church's leaders, at any level, must function with sensitivity to the culture and in doing so will give a much higher probability for growth.

It is basic to the functioning of leadership that they realize and understand that church growth is a process, not an event. Leaders and churches tend to be event-oriented in their programming and methodologies rather than process-oriented. In church growth there may be some important events, but no one event or combination of events will produce sustained church growth. Leaders must lead in that process. Delos Miles, in *Church Growth — A Mighty River*, has summed up the process as follows:

> *1. Because church growth is a process rather than an event; it requires planning — long-range planning, annual planning, and day-to-day planning.*

113

2. Because church growth is a process, it requires management of time, programs, personnel, materials, and so forth. The business world refers to this as MBO (Management by Objectives).

3. Because church growth is a process rather than an event, it involves setting objectives and goals and specific actions which can be measured and calendared.

4. Because church growth is a process, it is dynamic rather than static. It is flexible and fluid rather than set in concrete. It is forever changing and evolving.

5. Because church growth is a process, it interacts dynamically with culture. It never occurs in a cultural vacuum.

6. Because church growth is a process, it is not a gimmick. It is not a clever scheme to lift a church out of a numerical slump. It doesn't seek to "hook" persons through some cleverly devised manipulations of their psyche. Church growth exists for long-term gains and not just for short-term results.

7. Because church growth is a process, it must have a healthy respect for history. It takes the long look backward and forward. It sees the spiritual value of accurate records.

*8. Because church growth is a process, it is not a fad here today and gone tomorrow. There can be nothing effervescent about church growth. McGavran is only the father of the **modern** church growth movement. Even so, he has been working at it diligently for well over twenty years. If it were a fad, it might have flourished and perished twenty deaths in that many years. God, the heavenly Father, is really the Father of all genuine church growth.*

9. Because church growth is a process, it is not a program which you can pick up this fall and lay down next summer. Programs come and go, but a process starts and continues until its completion. You can't pick it up and lay it aside at your pleasure without suffering dire consequences.[15]

The leaders of the Church must function as a vital part of this church growth process. A number of leadership functions will now be explored that relate to that process.

Church leaders must demonstrate by their spiritual discipline, management of time, and lifestyle that they are aggressively committed to church growth. Authority is earned by the leadership who are willing to have church growth eyes to see the mission of the Church and can demonstrate the church growth message in life-related ministries. Leaders must by example exhibit a clear commitment to, and involvement in, the church growth process.

Church growth leadership must avoid the greatest pitfall of ministry — the syndrome of church development. For a leader in cross-cultural ministries it means that the new believers in the developing congregation must be allowed to develop their own relevant patterns of church organization, liturgy, leadership, finances, and training. Once the national church has come into being some missionaries may want to leave the concerns for evangelism and church growth to the nationals. The missionaries then get involved in teaching the Bible to the Christians, helping them raise better crops, improve their hygiene, train their pastors and a host of other good things.[16] Although aware of the purposes for which the Church was established, Church leaders and missionaries are nevertheless confronted constantly with the need for merely preserving the institution itself. But leaders, who are genuinely in tune with God's concern for growth, recognize that the Church exists to extend itself outside of its own walls.[17]

Another important function of the leadership is to communicate church growth to the believing community in every way possible. The Church's leaders must know where God wants the Church to go, how it is to grow, and the necessary steps that must be carried out.[18] The leadership must communicate church growth through preaching, teaching and attitude so that the congregation thinks growth. Social activities, athletic activities, meetings of all types, and worship services will be permeated by a growth mind-set in a growing congregation. Church growth must be communicated by the leadership to such a degree that it is more than a project, it is a way of thinking and living.

Church growth leaders, particularly pastors, must use their time wisely, for how a leader functions with available time has a great effect on the congregation's growth. Most leaders are not supervised in their use of time. Thus, it is urgent, and in good stewardship, for the Church's leadership to determine how much time should be alloted to various functions. It is most unfortunate that many congregations, in choosing a pastor, place greatest priority on the ability to preach. Certainly, congregations are entitled to well prepared and delivered messages from the Word. Yet, sermon delivery represents a very small portion of the pastor's total time for ministry. Indications are that the pulpit ministry, by itself, is a relatively minor factor in the growth of a congregation. A pastor's responsibilities, for example, include a wide variety of ministries. Research indicates that two particular pastoral ministries have a high degree of influence on church growth. The two growth producing ministries are visiting potential prospects and training laity for outreach. In four essentially identical congregations over a ten-year period the emphasis of each pastor had a particular effect on growth (Figure 5)[19] Thus, pastors and lay leaders need to distribute their time in such a way so that growth producing functions are given sufficient time involvement.

Church leaders cannot do all the Church must do. There are certain ministries that Church leaders must directly carry out. One of the primary tasks of the pastor is to equip the saints qualitatively so that the Church will grow quantitatively. The pastor must "become the coach of the team."[20] Many Christians are educated far beyond their level of obedience and are not translating Christian theory into practice. They know more about church policy than evangelism, and are better equipped with parliamentary procedure than with discipleship. It is impossible for a pastor and a few lay leaders to carry out all of the ministry functions given in the New Testament. Christ has raised up leadership in the Church for the purpose of helping every believer "discover, develop, and deploy his gifts[21] in ways that contribute to the welfare of the entire body and further

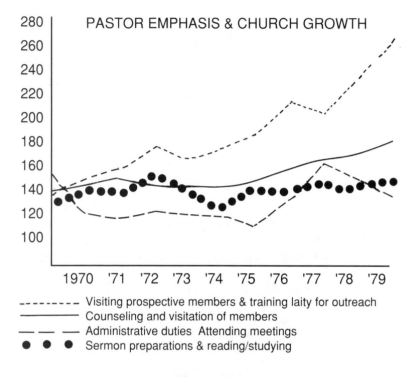

Figure 5[22]

God's mission in the world. Thus, the role of the leadership is not one of getting things done through people but one of developing the people of God so that their lives and ministries contribute to the qualitative and quantitative growth of the church. This is expertly summed up by David McKenna as he speaks, in particular, of the pastoral leadership role:

> *According to Ephesians 4:12, the gift of the pastor is given for the ". . . perfecting of the saints, for the work of the ministry, and the edifying of the body of Christ." As communicator, he equips the Body; as coordinator, he edifies the Body. What about the "work of the ministry?"* **Like the cerebellum, the pastor directs the Body as it responds to the external world.** *Of all social*

institutions, only the church has the primary purpose of
serving people who are not its members. Once again, we
are brought up short against the Great Commission.
When all is said and done, the pastor's responsibility for
equipping the saints and edifying the Body is for one,
high-intensity purpose — to evangelize the world. Every
pastor's performance will be judged on that bottom line.

   Body leadership saves the pastor from being either a
"balloon-holder" or a "shining star." Even the idea of
leader-follower is too bland to describe the strength and
the beauty of the relationship between a pastor and his
people in the Body of Christ. We need to rewrite the
leadership role of the pastor to be:

   — *Authoritative communicator of truth*
      for equipping the Body
   — *Efficient coordinator of functions*
      for edifying the Body
   — *Effective director of members*
      for evangelizing the world.

   The biblical role of the pastor is the resolution of the
leader-follower paradox.[23]

Another extremely important function of church growth leaders is to train leadership for growth. Denominational and mission leaders must train or see that their pastors and missionaries are schooled in church growth. Pastors and missionaries in turn are responsible to train lay leaders. When leaders at all of these levels are trained in church growth, the entire body can then be motivated and mobilized to be involved in the church growth process.[24] Since the local church is the area where growth actually occurs, the congregation is obligated to train its leadership. Church growth training materials are generally available through denominational or interdenominational sources. Possibilities for growth are bright if the local congregation recruits and trains its leadership in church growth. Denominations and independent organizations can assist in holding regional church growth seminars for the leaders of local churches. There is also an abundance of books and magazines that individual leaders can read to increase their knowledge and practical abilities in church growth. The leadership training must be of a particular type for leadership training comes with many different emphases. Leaders can be trained in many ways but the Church must be sure that its leaders are trained in church growth.[25] They must be trained so that they develop "church growth eyes."[26]

The pastor is not to be the only one doing the work of evangelism. He or she must aggressively train others to be involved in outreach. Good preaching does not generally attract the unsaved into the Church. However, the preaching and teaching of the pastor does contribute to the qualitative growth of the believers. Thus, it is the function of the pastor to train the believers, particularly key lay leaders, to do the work of evangelism.[27] Too many Christians have a knowledge of more Biblical truth than they are willing to obey. It is time that Christians be trained to be productive personal witnesses. Churches ought to consider revamping the mid-week service to give this kind of training to the believers. As they begin a more active personal witness they will automatically grow spiritually. As they breath out spiritually they will be eager to breath in spiritually. In addition to training the believers in personal witness, lay leaders must be trained in evangelism to lead structured outreach programs of the congregation. C. B. Hogue, in his book, *I Want My Church to Grow*, refers to this type of trained leaders as the "Evangelism Leadership Group." In order to highlight the importance of these trained lay leaders Hogue has also suggested a group commitment that would be signed by each member of the group (Figure 6).[28]

My personal commitment to growing my church:
I have studied carefully the theology and vision for growing an evangelistic church. I believe that God wants our church to grow both numerically and in the loving Christlike evangelistic ministry. Believing this, I make the following physical, emotional, intellectual, and spiritual commitment of myself to God and to growing this church.

119

1. I commit myself to be a witness in my life-style and to develop my own personal spiritual life through prayer, Bible study, and meditation.

2. I commit myself to a growing understanding of the theology and vision for growing Christ's church.

3. I commit myself to sharing the vision with individuals and groups within the church until the body of the church is permeated with a philosophy of church growth.

_____ Signed
_____ Date

The Evangelism Leadership Group will exchange this commitment page with other members of the group, and each person will sign as a commitment to one another.

Pastor _____   _____   _____

            _____   _____   _____

            _____   _____   _____

            _____   _____   _____

            _____   _____   _____

            _____   _____   _____

            _____   _____   _____

Figure 6 Evangelism Leadership
Group Commitment[29]

In conjuntion with the training of leadership in the church growth process, there must also be a definite plan to carry out growth projections. The function of leadership is to develop a plan whereby a specific strategy is developed that is carried out through leadership management. This can and should be done by the denominational and mission leaders in general terms, and more importantly at the local level in each congregation. The Church is God's work. The Church therefore deserves the best of our planning efforts that are based on sound growth projections. This practice "should be instilled in each new church that comes into being and needs to be taught to the older churches that have forgotten or ignored" it.[30] Goals (discussed earlier in the chapter) and plans must go together. Plans communicate clear intentions as to how the leadership is going to lead in order to accomplish the goals. Time spent in planning is good stewardship of the growth opportunities that the Church faces. Church growth is important enough to plan for it. "Too often in the church today **problem solving** takes the place of **goal setting**."[31] Planning must be thought of as a bridge between where the congregation is in its present quantitative and qualitative growth and the growth goal they believe God wants them to achieve. Goals and planning can and should be coordinated by the leadership. Spiritually sensitive Christians from within a congregation will also be able to contribute ideas for the goals and plans for growth.[32] Growth of any significant degree does not just happen. Significant church growth is planned for. Growth is almost guaranteed when leaders plan for it and then aggressively work for it.

The Church's leadership also functions for the cause of church growth by using various methodologies. One large area of the planning process is to develop specific tailor-made methodologies for growth. The leadership must aggressively experiment with all kinds of methods for enhancing the growth of the congregation. There is, of course, always a chance of making mistakes in methodology. The perceptive leadership consistently reviews and revises each method to achieve maximum results. Some methods will work in one location and will not work in another. It is extremely important for the leadership to perceptively find the particular methodologies for their particular congregation that work in that particular community.[33] Church growth will be stagnant or slow if the leadership perpetuates programs and methodologies that are complicated and ineffectual. The congretaion will be less motivated for church growth when the program or methodology is too complex. The leadership will be wise to design simple programming and methodologies that everyone can understand and in which everyone can become involved.[34]

Lastly, it is the function of the Church's leadership to keep accurate records of every facet of the denomination and congregation. Accurate records give a clear picture of where the Church has been, where it is at the moment, and where the Church may or should grow in the future with God's help. Every aspect of the Church's life that can be quantified should be recorded. Just as a medical doctor takes numerous measurements to get an overall picture of a person's health, the Church must continually take accurate measurements to monitor its health. Quantitative measurements generally give a rather clear picture of the qualitative growth or health of the Church. Bob Wagmire and C. Peter Wagner have prepared an excellent step-by-step workbook that the Church's leadership can use to chart, measure, and analyze churches in a geographical area, a special group of churches, or a local congregation. With such a practical research tool available there is no excuse for the leadership not to be analyzing the Church's growth and charting its future potential. Another church growth research instrument, which has been translated in a number of third world languages, is Vergil Gerber's *God's Way to Keep a Church Going & Growing*. This book gives a brief summary of church growth concepts and then a step-by-step procedure for charting the Church's growth. The bottom line is that there is no excuse for the leadership to not be knowledgeable of church growth and actually know the growth picture in every single congregation.

---

[1] Howard A. Snyder, *The Problem of Wine Skins: Church Structure in a Technological Age* (Downers Grove: InterVarsity Press, 1975), p. 84.

[2] McGavran and Arn, *How to Grow a Church*, p. 83.

[3] Wagner, *Your Church Can Grow*, pp. 30-31.

[4] Herb Miller, *Evangelism's Open Secrets* (St. Louis: The Bethany Press, 1977), pp. 62-63.

[5] Wagner, *Your Church Can Grow*, p. 56.

[6] Sanders, *Spiritual Leadership*, p. 35.

[7] Ibid., p. 34.

[8] Miller, *Evangelism's Open Secret*, p. 57.

[9]Dudley, *Where Have All Our People Gone?*, pp. 106-07, 114.

[10]Wagner, *Your Church Can Grow*, p. 57.

[11]Win Arn, "How to Find a Pastor Who Fits Your Church . . . or How to Find a Church That Fits You," in *The Pastor's Church Growth Handbook*, ed. Win Arn (Pasadena: Church Growth Press, 1979), pp. 12-13.

[12]Bartel, *A New Look at Church Growth*, pp. 68-69.

[13]Wagner, *Your Church Can Grow*, pp. 30-31.

[14]Charles H. Kraft, *Christianity in Culture* (MaryKnoll, N.Y.: Orbis Books, 1979), p. 321.

[15]Miles, *Church Growth — A Mighty River*, pp. 86-87.

[16]C. Peter Wagner, "The Danger of a Truncated Missionary Goal," *Evangelical Missions Quarterly* 9 (Winter 1973):95, 99.

[17]Anderson and Jones, *The Management of Ministry*, p. 8.

[18]Wagner, *Your Church Can Be Healthy*, p. 106.

[19]Arn, "How to Find a Pastor Who Fits Your Church . . . or How to Find a Church That Fits You," pp. 12, 14.

[20]Wagner, *Your Spiritual Gifts Can Help Your Church Grow*, p. 165.

[21]Adams, *Pastoral Leadership*, p. 13.

[22]Arn, "How to Find a Pastor Who Fits Your Church . . . or How to Find a Church That Fits You," p. 14.

[23]David L. McKenna, "The Ministry's Gordian Knot," *Leadership* 1 (Winter 1980):51.

[24]Chapter five covered the issue of theological education that includes church growth training.

[25]McGavran and Arn, *How to Grow a Church*, pp. 79-80, 108.

[26]McGavran and Arn in *Ten Steps for Church Growth* define "church growth eyes" as: "a characteristic of Christians who have achieved an ability to see the possibilities for growth and to apply appropriate strategies to gain maximum results for Christ and His Church," p. 127.

[27]McGavran and Arn, *How to Grow a Church*, p. 86.

[28]Hogue, *I Want My Church to Grow*, p. 160.

[39]Ibid.

[30]Lockwood, "Assimilating New Members," p. 155.

[31]Riggs, *Make It Happen*, p. 45.

[32]Edward R. Dayton and David A. Fraser, *Planning Strategies for World Evangelization* (Grand Rapids: William B. Eerdmans Publishing Company, 1980), pp. 444-45.

[33] Miller, *Evangelism's Open Secrets*, p. 61.

[34]Green, *Why Churches Die: A Guide to Basic Evangelism and Church Growth*, p. 36.

CHAPTER VIII

The Challenge Of Leadership In Church Growth

Immense Responsibility Of Leadership In Church Growth

"The success or failure, the rise and fall of groups and organizations, be they religious or secular, is determined by the quality of leadership."[1] "When God has a job to do He places His hand upon a man."[2] It is clear that the leaders of the Church have an awesome responsibility, particularly in the area of church growth. Leaders have the responsibility to equip the saints and to build the congregation both spiritually and numerically.

Leadership is a key, if not the key, of church growth. Churches grow or stagnate or die because of their leadership. When God wants to build His Church, He always begins with a person, a person with a vision and a burden, a person with a deep desire to honor the Lord, a passion to lead others to Him, and to follow the principles of church growth.

Some may say that we "are not commanded to be fruitful, but to be faithful."[3] Tippett, in his book *Church Growth and the Word of God*, rejects this distinction. The word

125

"faithful" has several meanings. One of its meanings is "fruit-ful."[4] It involves being faithful through being fruitful. Scripture gives overwhelming evidence that God demands responsibility from those who serve, and that includes the expectation of results from the servant's work. God clearly expects His leaders of the Church to be informed of, concerned for, and involved in church growth. A leader who is faithful will be fruitful for the cause of church growth.

It is possible that leaders can actually obstruct the growth of the Church. The greatest hindrance may be the attitude, "whatever will be will be." Church growth that is pleasing to God and pushes back the enemy will never happen unless the leadership of the Church works aggressively for it. Even if the Church's leadership holds to sound evangelical theology, growth will not occur unless there are concrete efforts. The people in the pews are ready to be led. If the Church's leadership will point the way, and not get in the way, the Church will grow.

The responsibility of the Church's leadership is immense. The leadership will generally center its attention on one of three legitimate areas of concern. The tendency of too many leaders is to be involved in the maintenance of the Church that already exists. Another area of leadership involvement is in problem-solving. There is the tendency for a few leaders to get bogged down in putting out "fires" in the Church. And then lastly there is the area of church growth. Fortunately more and more leaders are steering their attention to church growth as an orientation of their ministry.

Great Opportunity For Leadership
In Church Growth

History can provide a good lesson in how leadership affects church growth. Jonathan Chao has identified seven secrets of church growth in China. He noted that the key element of the Church's growth may well be the many Christian leaders

126

who have had a long and consistent history of obedience under persecution. By contrast it is well documented that during the militaristic era in Japan the Church's leadership compromised their obedience to Christ. Under pressure from the government almost all pastors, with the exception of some in the Holiness Churches, bowed to the tablets of the Emperor and gave silent assent to the militarist policies. When Japan was finally defeated, and the Emperor denied his divinity, the people's spirit was severely broken and receptive to the certainty of the Gospel. But the Church's leadership had no message for them. They had lost credibility and, as a result, church growth suffered.[5]

Christians in general, and Christian leaders specifically, must see that they stand on the edge of the greatest expansion of the Church the world has ever seen. Some are saying that the world has entered a post-Christian era. Yet the facts clearly indicate that the Church is expanding around the world, and will continue to do so.[6]

Win Arn has given the following four reasons why he believes that in the next five, ten, twenty years there will be an unprecedented advance of the Church around the world:

1. Church Growth thinking finds its basic reason for existence in God's unswerving purpose — the redemption of lost mankind. When this purpose is understood and acted upon in the most strategic and effective ways, God's blessing and a growing church are to be expected.

2. A large number of dedicated Christians, both lay and clergy, are being trained in the expanding knowledge coming from the study of growing churches. These individuals are discovering that, through the application of Church Growth principles, their churches can be more successful in winning lost people to Jesus Christ and building them into the church's fellowship.

3. Church Growth thinking brings a new dimension for the church . . . a new perspective or frame of reference for seeing the church. Church Growth does not mean a program of evangelism, door-to-door visitation, or phone calling. It is rather a way of looking at a church, as it is obedient — or disobedient — to Christ's command to "Go and make disciples." Church Growth then develops strategy to identify the ways each church can be most effective in reaching the unchurched in its ministry area. We call this perspective, "Seeing through Church Growth Eyes."

4. Results are achieved. Pastors and people applying growth principles see results . . . "God gives the increase."[7]

There is no special methodology that will produce an "instant church." In the twentieth century with emphasis on comfort, it may be hard for some to realize that churches are planted and grow through disciplined effort. Vergil Gerber summed it up well:

Even after two thousand years of Christian experience and evangelistic know-how in the ecclesiastical science of church-birth, there are still no easy formulas nor simple how-to-do-it package plans for church reproduction. Winston Churchill's pungent words, "blood, sweat and tears," serve to remind us that the church too is born of blood, sweat and tears — the blood of Christ, the sweat of discipleship and the tears of prevailing prayer.[8]

Great stress today is laid on money and methods but God still works through individuals to bring growth to the Church. God works through the human servant.[9] As the Church's leadership develops "church growth eyes" and sees the possibilities, as it discovers methods that prove effective and discard methods that are clearly ineffective, the Church will experience greater growth than ever before. The goal is that there be a church in every people group of the world. Every society should be able to witness genuine Christian life where there are groups of committed Christians who are loving, serving, praying, growing in the Word, and reaching out.

The Church's leadership is therefore presented with a matchless opportunity to lead the way to unprecedented church growth.

---

[1]Wolff, *Man at the Top*, p. 2.

[2]Harold L. Fickett, Jr., *Hope for Your Church* (Glendale, Calif.: Regal Books, 1972). p. ii.

[3]Tippett, *Church Growth and the Word of God*, p. 40.

[4]Ibid.

[5]"Faithful Suffering and Church Growth," *China Prayer News,*, February 1983, p. 3.

[6]McGavran and Arn, *Ten Steps for Church Growth*, p. 19.

[7]Win Arn, "People Are Asking . . ." in *The Pastor's Church Growth Handbook*, ed. Win Arn (Pasadena: Church Growth Press, 1979), p. 200.

[8]Gerber, "Starting and Organizing Local Churches Overseas," p. 30.

[9]Ibid., p. 36.

Bibliography

Adams, Arthur Merrihew. *Pastoral Administration*. Philadelphia: The Westminster Press, 1964.

Adams, Jay E. *Pastoral Leadership*. Grand Rapids: Baker Book House, 1975.

Anderson, James D., and Jones, Ezra Earl. *The Management of Ministry*. San Francisco: Harper & Row, 1978.

Arn, Win. "How to Find a Pastor Who Fits Your Church . . . or How to Find a Church That Fits You." In *The Pastor's Church Growth Handbook*, pp. 7-14. Edited by Win Arn. Pasadena: Church Growth Press, 1979.

_____. "People Are Asking . . ." In *The Pastor's Church Growth Handbook*, pp. 198-205. Edited by Win Arn. Pasadena: Church Growth Press, 1979.

Bartel, Floyd G. *A New Look at Church Growth*. Newton, Kan.: Faith and Life Press, 1979.

Belew, M. Wendell. *Churches and How They Grow*. Nashville: Broadman Press, 1971.

Bohren, Rudolf. *Preaching and Community*. Richmond, Va.: John Knox Press, 1965.

Campbell, Thomas C. *The Gift of Administration*. Philadelphia: The Westminster Press, 1981.

Chandapilla, P. T. "How to Develop Indian Leaders." *Evangelical Missions Quarterly* 5 (Spring 1969):151-62.

Chaney, Charles L., and Lewis, Ron S. *Design for Church Growth*. Nashville: Broadman, 1977.

Coleman, Robert E. *The Master Plan of Evangelism*. Old Tappen, N.J.: Fleming H. Revell Company, 1972.

_____. "The Master's Plan." In *Perspectives on the World Christian Movement*, pp. 70-74. Edited by Ralph D. Winter and Steve C. Hawthorne. Pasadena: William Carey Library, 1981.

Cook, Harold R. *Historic Patterns of Church Growth*. Chicago: Moody Press, 1971.

Currin, James H. "The Leadership of Churches." In *The Birth of Churches*, pp. 123-37. Edited by Talmadge R. Amberson. Nashville: Broadman, 1979.

Dayton, Edward R., and Fraser, David A. *Planning Strategies For World Evangelization*. Grand Rapids: William B. Eerdmans Publishing Company, 1980.

"Denominational Executives Can Stimulate Growth." *Net Results*, February 1981, Vol. 1, no. 7, pp. 1, 4.

Dobbins, Gaines S. *Building Better Churches*. Nashville: Broadman Press, 1947.

Dubose, Francis M. *How Churches Grow in an Urban World*. Nashville: Broadman Press, 1978.

Dudley, Carl S. *Where Have All Our People Gone?* New York: The Pilgrim Press, 1979.

Eims, LeRoy. *Be the Leaders You Were Meant to Be*. Wheaton: Victor Books, 1975.

Emery, O. D. *Concepts to Grow By*. Marion, Ind.: The Wesley Press, 1976.

English, John Mahan. *The Minister and His Ministry*. Philadelphia: The Judson Press, 1924.

Engstrom, Theodore Whilhelm, and Dayton, Edward R. *The Art of Management for Christian Leaders*. Waco: Word Books, Publisher, 1976.

"Faithful Suffering and Church Growth." *China Prayer News*, February 1983, p. 3.

Fickett, Harold C. Jr. *Hope for Your Church*. Glendale, Calif.: Regal Books, 1972.

Flynn, Leslie B. *19 Gifts of the Spirit*. Wheaton: Victor Books, 1974.

Gangel, Kenneth. "Laying a Biblical Foundation." In *Church Leadership Development*, pp. 15-30. Edited by Scripture Press Ministries. Glen Ellyn, Ill.: Scripture Press Ministries, 1977.

Gerber, Vergil. *God's Way to Keep a Church Going & Growing*. South Pasadena: William Carey Library, 1973.

_____. "Starting and Organizing Local Churches Overseas." *Evangelical Missions Quarterly* 6 (Fall 1969):28-37.

Gibbs, Eddie. "Optimism Spreads in British Churches." *Global Church Growth Bulletin* 18 (March-April 1981): 95-96; 107.

Green, Hollis L. *Why Churches Die: A Guide to Basic Evangelism and Church Growth*. Minneapolis: Bethany Fellowship, 1972.

Green, Michael. *Evangelism in the Early Church*. Grand Rapids: William B. Eerdmans Publishing Company, 1970.

Griffiths, Michael. *The Church & World Mission*. Grand Rapids: Zondervan Publishing House, 1980.

Hedlund, Roger E. "Why Do Churches in India Grow?" *Asia Theological News*, July-September 1982, pp. 10-11, 19.

Hendricks, Howard, ed. "The Missing Ingredient: Leadership Training," *Partners*, October/November/December 1982, pp. 11-13.

Hesselgrave, David J. *Planting Churches Cross-Culturally: A Guide for Home and Foreign Missions*. Grand Rapids: Baker Book House, 1980.

Hesselgrave, David J., ed. *Dynamic Religious Movements*. Grand Rapids: Baker Book House, 1978.

Hillard, Mahlon. "Mark Twain and the Leadership Church." *The Standard*, May 1, 1973, p. 27.

Hodges, Melvin L. *The Indigenous Church*. Springfield, Mo.: Gospel Publishing House, 1953.

Hogue, C. B. *I Want My Church to Grow*. Nashville: Broadman, 1977.

Huffman, John; De Witt, Larry; Eller, Vernard; Huffman, John A. Jr.; Patterson, Ben; and Wagner, C. Peter. "Leadership Forum: Must a Healthy Church Be a Growing Church?" *Leadership* 2 (Winter 1981):127-38.

Hutcheson, Richard G. *Wheel Within the Wheel: Confronting the Management Crisis of the Pluralistic Church*. Atlanta: John Knox Press, 1979.

Keating, Charles J. *The Leadership Book*. New York: Paulist Press, 1978.

Kinsler, F. Ross. *The Extension Movement in Theological Education*. Pasadena: William Carey Library, 1978.

Kraemer, Hendrik. *The Christian Message in a Non-Christian World*. Grand Rapids: Kregel Publications, 1938.

Kraft, Charles II. *Christianity in Culture*. MaryKnoll, N.Y.: Orbis Books, 1979.

Latourette, Kenneth Scott. *A History of the Expansion of Christianity*. 7 vols. New York: Harper & Brothers, 1937-1945.

Lawson, E. LeRoy. *Church Growth: Everybody's Business*. Cincinnati: Standard Publishing, 1975.

Lebsack, Lee. *Ten at the Top*. Stow, Ohio: New Hope Press, 1974.

LePeau, Andrew T. *Paths of Leadership*. Downers Grove: InterVarsity Press, 1983.

Lockwood, Quentin. "The Growth of Churches." In *The Birth of Churches*, pp. 152-62. Edited by Talmadge R. Amberson. Nashville: Broadman, 1979.

McGavran, Donald A. *Understanding Church Growth*. Grand Rapids: William B. Eerdmans Publishing Company, 1980.

McGavran, Donald A., and Arn, Win C. *How To Grow A Church*. Glendale, Calif.: Regal Books, 1973.

McGavran, Donald A., and Arn, Winfield C. *Ten Steps for Church Growth*. New York: Harper & Row, Publishers, 1977.

McGavran, Donald and Hunter, George G. III. *Church Growth Strategies that Work*. Nashville: Abingdon, 1980.

133

McKenna, Daivd L. "The Ministry's Gordian Knot." *Leadership* 1 (Winter 1980):45-51.

McKinney, Lois. "Leadership: Key to the Growth of the Church." In *Discipling through Theological Education by Extension*, pp. 179-91. Edited by Vergil Gerber. Chicago: Moody Press, 1980.

_____. "Plan for the Church's Leadership Needs." *Evangelical Missions Quarterly* 11 (July 1975):183-87.

_____. "Theological Education Overseas: A Church-Centered Approach." Paper presented at the 37th annual meeting of the National Association of Evangelicals, Orlando, Fla., 6-8 March 1979. (Mimeographed.)

Mercaldo, Daniel; Finks, Frederick J.; and Pohl, Wayne A. "Growth Around the World: Growing Churches in the USA." *Global Church Growth Bulletin* 18 (September-October 1981):139-40.

Miles, Delos. *Church Growth — A Mighty River*. Nashville: Broadman Press, 1981.

Miller, Ernest. "Church Growth Compared to Caterpillar." *Net Results*, December 1980, p. 3.

Miller, Herb. *Evangelism's Open Secrets*. St. Louis: The Bethany Press, 1977.

Minnery, Thomas A. "Success in Three Churches: Diversity and Originality." *Leadership* 2 (Winter 1981):57-65.

Miranda, Juan Carlos. " 'Rosario' Came Just in Time." *Church Growth Bulletin* 14 (September 1977):150-51.

Missionary News Service. 1 December 1982, Vol. 30, No. 3.

Mylander, Charles. *Secrets for Growing Churches*. San Francisco: Harper & Row, Publishers, 1979.

Neill, Stephen. *A History of Christian Missions*. Baltimore: Penguin Books, 1964.

Nelson, Marlin L. "Korea: Asia's First Christian Nation?" *Asia Theological News* 8 (July-September 1982):14-15.

Nida, Eugene A. *Message and Mission*. New York: Harper & Row Publishers, 1960.

Norish, A. E. *Give Us Men*. Dorset, England: The Overcomer Literature Trust, n.d.

Olley, John W. "Leadership: Some Biblical Perspectives." *The South East Asia Journal of Theology* 18 (No. 1-1977):1-20.

Orjala, Paul R. *Get Ready to Grow: A Strategy for Local Church Growth*. Kansas City: Beacon Hill Press of Kansas City, 1978.

Pentecost, Edward C. *Issues in Missiology: An Introduction*. Grand Rapids: Baker Book House, 1982.

Peters, George W. *A Theology of Church Growth*. Grand Rapids: Zondervan Publishing House, 1981.

Powell, Paul W. *How to Make Your Church Hum*. Nashville: Broadman Press, 1977.

Powers, Bruce P. *Christian Leadership*. Nashville: Broadman, 1979.

Rambo, David Lloyd. "Training Competent Leaders for the Christian and Missionary Alliance Churches of the Philippines." M.A. thesis, Fuller Theolgical Seminary, 1968.

Riggs, Donald E. *Make it Happen*. Warsaw, Ind.: LP Publications, 1981.

Ro, Bong Rin. "Seven Issues in Asian Theological Education." *Asian Missions Advance* 8 (July 1979):1-3.

Ro, Bong Rin, ed. "Crisis in the Local Church." *Asia Theological News*, July-September 1982, pp. 3-13.

Robertson, Deanna Ruth. "A Study of Leadership Style: A Comparison of Secular and Biblical Settings." M.B.A. thesis, Oral Roberts University, 1980.

Sanders, J. Oswald. *Spiritual Leadership*. Chicago: Moody Press, 1967.

Saracco, J. Norberto. "The Type of Ministry Adopted by the Pentecostal Churches in Latin America." *International Review of Missions* 66 (January 1977):64-70.

Schaller, Lyle E. *Assimilating New Members*. Nashville: Abingdon, 1978.

_____. *The Change Agent*. Nashville: Abingdon, 1972.

_____. "The Changing Focus of Church Finances." *Leadership* 2 (Spring 1981):12-24.

_____. *The Multiple Staff and the Larger Church*. Nashville: Abingdon, 1980.

Shawchuck, Norman. "Church Management: The Architecture of Ministry." *Christianity Today* 23 (July 1979):19-22.

Smylie, James H. "Church Growth and Decline in Historical Perspective: Protestant Quest for Identity, Leadership, and Meaning." In *Understanding Church Growth and Decline, 1950-1979*, pp. 69-93. Edited by Dean R. Hoge and David A. Roozen. New York: Pilgrim Press, 1979.

Snyder, Howard A. *The Problem of Wine Skins: Church Structure in a Technological Age*. Downers Grove: InterVarsity Press, 1975.

Swanson, Allen J., ed. *I Will Build My Church: Ten Case Studies of Church Growth in Taiwan*. Pasadena: William Carey Library, 1977.

Swindoll, Charles R. *Hand Me Another Brick*. Nashville: Thomas Nelson Publishers, 1978.

Takami, Toshihiro. "Concepts of Leadership and Their Meaning for the Growth of Christian Churches." M.A. thesis, Fuller Theological Seminary, 1969.

The Christian and Missionary Alliance. "Lima Hosts Alliance World Fellowship." *Alliance World Prayer Line*, March 1983, p. 1.

_____. "New Hope for Dying Churches." *Open Line*, July-August 1982, p. 3.

Tippett, A. R. *Church Growth and the Word of God*. Grand Rapids: William B. Eerdmans Publishing Company, 1970.

Towns, Elmer L. *Getting a Church Started in the Face of Insurmountable Odds with Limited Resources in Unlikely Circumstances*. Nashville: Impact Books, 1975.

Uhlig, John. "Growth-Restricting Obstacles: How to Find and Overcome Them." In *The Pastor's Church Growth Handbook*, pp. 69-75. Edited by Win Arn. Pasadena: Church Growth Press, 1979.

Wagner, C. Peter. "Good Pastors Don't Make Churches Grow." *Leadership* 2 (Winter 1981):66-72.

_____. *Stop the World I Want to Get On*. Glendale, Calif.: Regal Books, 1974.

_____. "The Danger of a Truncated Missionary Goal." *Evangelical Missions Quarterly* 9 (Winter 1973):94-100.

_____. *Your Church Can Be Healthy*. Nashville: Abingdon, 1979.

_____. *Your Church Can Grow*. Glendale, Calif.: Regal Books, 1976.

_____. *Your Spiritual Gifts Can Help Your Church Grow*. Glendale, Calif.: Regal Books, 1974.

Ward, Ted. "Facing Educational Issues." In *Church Leadership Development*, pp. 31-46. Edited by Scripture Press Ministries. Glen Ellyn, Ill.: Scripture Press Ministries, 1977.

_____. "Servants, Leaders and Tyrants." Paper presented at Calvin Theological Seminary, Grand Rapids, Mich., 29 March 1978. (Mimeographed.)

Wolff, Richard. *Man at the Top*. Wheaton: Tyndale House Publishers, 1969.

Womack, David A. *The Pyramid Principle of Church Growth*. Minneapolis: Bethany Fellowship, Inc., 1977.

Wong, James. "Training of the Ministry for Rapid Church Growth." In *Voice of the Church in Asia*, pp. 77-80. Edited by Asia Theological Association. Hong Kong: Christian Communications Ltd., 1975.

Yeo, Aldred C. H. "Singapore's Secret of Success." *Asia Theological News*, July-September 1982, pp. 18-19.

Young, J. Terry. "The Holy Spirit and the Birth of Churches." In *The Birth of Churches*, pp. 163-79. Edited by Talmadge R. Amberson. Nashville: Broadman, 1979.